LIVING IN THE CITY
ЖИЗНЬ В ГОРОДЕ
VIVRE DANS LA VILLE
LEBEN IN DER STADT

EUROPEAN COMMISSION - DIRECTORATE GENERAL XII FOR SCIENCE RESEARCH AND DEVELOPMENT
ЕВРОПЕЙСКОЙ КОМИССИИ - XII ДИРЕКТОРАТА ПО НАУЧНЫМ ИССЛЕДОВАНИЯМ И РАЗВИТИЮ
COMMISSION EUROPEENNE - DIRECTION GENERALE XII POUR LA SCIENCE, LA RECHERCHE ET LE DEVELOPPEMENT
EUROPÄISCHE KOMISSION - GENERALDIREKTION XII FÜR WISSENSCHAFT, FORSCHUNG UND ENTWICKLUNG

LIVING IN THE CITY

Published for European Commission Directorate General XII
for Science, Research and Development by the
Energy Research Group, University College Dublin

© Compilation copyright Energy Research Group,
  University College Dublin, 1996. All rights reserved.

Edited by Vivienne Brophy, John Goulding, J Owen Lewis

ISBN 1-898473-30-7

EUR 16657

ENERGY RESEARCH GROUP
School of Architecture, University College Dublin
Richview, Clonskeagh Drive, Dublin 14, Ireland
tel + 353 1 269 2750 / fax + 353 1 283 8908

Produced by Gandon Editions, Oysterhaven, Kinsale, Co Cork
tel + 353 21 770 830 / fax 770 755
Designed by John O'Regan (© Gandon, 1996)
Production by Nicola Dearey, Gandon

Photography by Gerry Hayden, UCD

Cover illustration by WH Hastings.

Printed and bound in Ireland by Betaprint, Dublin

ACKNOWLEDGEMENTS

This competition was arranged within the JOULE programme's
INNOBUILD project of the European Commission Directorate General
XII for Science, Research and Development. The project was super-
vised by Dr Georges Deschamps at the Commission.

INNOBUILD is co-ordinated by Prof. Owen Lewis at University
College Dublin. The competition was arranged by John Goulding,
assisted by Vivienne Brophy, at the Energy Research Group,
University College Dublin.

The following Task Group advised on the competition condi-
tions and its structure: Dr Nick Baker and Dr. Koen Steemers,
Cambridge; Elisabeth Friedemann, Berlin; Dr Zdravko Genchev, Sofia;
Poul Kristensen, Copenhagen; Shane O'Toole, Dublin; János Szász,
Pécs.

The Jury members for the competition were: Henri Ciriani,
Paris; Thomas Herzog, Munich; Jan Kaplicky, London; Henning
Larsen, Copenhagen; Alexandros Tombazis, Athens.

The Jury members reviewed the Competition Rules, Brief and
Conditions, as did the Commission on International Competitions, of
the Union International des Architects, Paris.

The Technical Assessors for the competition were: Dr Nick
Baker, Cambridge (joint chairman); Poul Kristensen, Copenhagen
(joint chairman); Dr Costas Balaras, Athens; Dr Elena Bazhenova,
Moscow; Eric Durand, Vendome; Dr Bob Everett, Cambridge; Paola
Fragnito, Milan; Dr Andreas Hänel, Munich; Paul Leech, Dublin;
Antonella Marucco, Torino; Emilio M. Mitre, Valladolid; Simon
O'Brien, Dublin; Dr Koen Steemers, Cambridge; János Szász, Pécs;
Dr Martin de Witt, Eindhoven

The LT4 Method and LT4 Method Guidelines were devised and
written by Dr Nick Baker and Dr Koen Steemers, Cambridge. Artwork
for worksheets, tables and figures was prepared by Michael Baker,
Cambridge.

The Design Guidelines were prepared by the Energy Research
Group, University College Dublin.

Information on the four default sites was assembled by: Dr
Elena Bazhenova (Moscow); Elisabeth Friedemann (Berlin); Dr
Zdravko Genchev (Bourgas); János Szász (Pécs).

Translation of the text from English to the other official lan-
guages of the competition was carried out by: Christoph
Brandstaetter (German); Eric Durand (French); Alexander Khrustalev
(Russian).

Graphic design work was carried out by ARC Survey Photo
Graphic Limited (Bill Hastings, John Kelly and David Cullivan), and
Pierre Jolivet. The documentation was printed by Lantz Ltd. and
Reprint Ltd., with the help of Lithographic Plate Plan Ltd.

Administrative and secetarial support were provided by Mary
Rigby, Martina McTeigue and Liz Mellon.

The exhibition of entries for assessment was organised by
Vivienne Brophy, assisted by Laughlin Rigby.

The prize-giving ceremony on 13 November 1995 and exhibition
of entries from 13 to 20 November 1995 at the School of
Architecture, University College Dublin were organised by Vivienne
Brophy, assisted by Laughlin Rigby, Rachel Byrne and Gavin
Wheatley.

CONTENTS

1   Prof J Owen Lewis, Director, Energy Research Group at the prize-giving ceremony in the School of Architecture, University College Dublin

2   Mr Paul Gormley, European Commission Representation in Ireland, with first-prize winners in the Architect section – Jean François Perretant, Frank Le Bail and Amilcar Dos Santos, Lyon

3   First-prize winners in the Student section – Kai Hansen and Stephanie Heese, Berlin

4   Exhibition at the Moscow Architectural Institute

5   Exhibition at the Moscow Architectural Institute

6   Exhibition at the Reabilitação Energética de Edifícios Workshop in Évora, Portugal

1

2

3

4

5

6

PREFACE

During the past two decades, the European Commission has strongly supported a wide range of R+D and dissemination activities to improve the energy efficiency and environmental performance of our buildings, which account for almost half of Europe's total energy use and consequent atmospheric pollution.

Many techniques, new building products and much design assistance are now available to assist architects and building engineers in making better buildings and more accurately predicting their performance at the design stage. However, the slow replacement rate of Europe's building stock, particularly in the extensive residential sector, requires that the performance of existing buildings is improved. The potential energy savings and environmental improvements from upgrading existing buildings are enormous.

To achieve large-scale energy savings, it is vital that decision makers in the main stream of building practice are aware of the architectural, environmental and economic possibilities of energy technologies for upgrading existing buildings. Appropriate design information and details of exemplary solutions applied to buildings in similar circumstances can be of enormous benefit to designers embarking on building retrofit projects.

Living in the City, the fifth architectural ideas competition promoted by the European Commission, has provided an exceptional opportunity to interest a wide audience in eastern and western Europe in the energy and environmental improvements which are possible when remodelling post-War apartment buildings. Furthermore, the wealth of architectural and technical ideas evident in the resulting competition entries represents a considerable source of inspiration to building designers faced with a similar design task.

This book documents the winning entries in the *Living in the City* competition, organised in 1994 and 1995 by the Energy Research Group, University College Dublin on behalf of the European Commission. It celebrates the excellence with which this rather complex challenge has been met by students and architects from every Member State and most other European countries. The aim of the book is now to spread this interest and knowledge to a larger audience. The Commission looks forward with confidence to the continued growth of interest and the consequent wide adaptation of these principles in building design throughout Europe.

Dr GEORGES DESCHAMPS
European Commission Directorate General XII
for Science, Research and Development

1 Novae Architectes, first-prize winners, Architect section

2 Sandrine Jourdain and Olivier Molla, second-prize winners, Architect section

3 Harri Hagan, third-prize winner, Architect section, with Paul Gormley, European Commission and John Goulding, Energy Research Group

4 Félix Jové Sandoval, joint fourth-prize winner, Architect section

5 Pierre Drolez and Elisabeth Lemercier, joint fourth-prize winners, Architect section

1

2

4

3

5

1   Kai Hansen and Stephanie Heese, first prize-winners, Student
    section.

2   Laurie Baggett and Kristian Uthe-Spencker, second-prize winners,
    Student section, with Paul Gormley, European Commission

3   Petteri Piha, third-prize winner, Student section, with Paul
    Gormley, European Commission

4   Dr Art Cosgrove, President of University College Dublin welcoming
    guests at the prize-giving ceremony in the School of Architecture,
    University College Dublin

5   Eva Förster, Richard Guy and Vincent Andrieu, fourth-prize
    winners, Student section, with Paul Gormley, European
    Commission

1

2

3

4

5

1 Competition announcements

2 Technical Assessors at work

3 Members of the Jury at work

4 Information pack for competitors

5 Technical Assessors at work

6 Members of the Jury at work

1

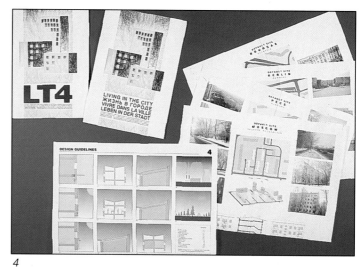

4

2

5

3

6

REGISTRAR'S REPORT

INTRODUCTION

This book contains the award-winning designs of the fifth EC international architectural ideas competition, announced in November 1995, for the remodelling and upgrading of multi-family apartment buildings constructed in the past five decades in Europe and for the innovative application of conservation technologies using passive solar heating, passive cooling and daylighting. The competition was open to all architects and architectural students resident within the European Union, the European Free Trade Area, and many of the new democracies of central and eastern Europe.

Living in the City was the fifth in a series of competitions sponsored by the European Commission, Directorate General XII for Science Research and Development, and the third organised by the Energy Research Group, University College Dublin. The first two focused on housing, while the third, *Working in the City* encouraged architects to consider the potential of passive solar design principles in offices and workplaces, with special emphasis on daylighting. The fourth, *Zephyr* focused on natural cooling and encouraged architects and engineers to find ways of creating comfort indoors in southern climates, without recourse to mechanical air conditioning.

After the Second World War, many European countries faced an acute housing problem. The requirements of short construction times, low costs and industrialised production led to mass-construction of pre-fabricated concrete buildings. Unrealistically low energy prices and lack of appropriate materials has, in some regions, often resulted in buildings with low levels of thermal insulation, inadequate means of regulating comfort levels and little individual metering or billing of energy consumption, leading to very high energy use in buildings.

About 40% of total energy consumption in Europe is used in buildings, many of which are large apartment buildings made of pre-fabricated components. Large numbers are in need of major renovation due to poor construction quality or deterioration with age, and the potential for energy savings is huge. If energy saving measures are combined with general renovation to improve amenity, then costs and pay-back periods can be reduced significantly.

Between 1945 and 1975, approximately ten million apartment units were constructed in the then European Community. If a figure of 500 ECU is taken as the average annual energy cost for each apartment, then a relatively modest reduction of 20% in energy consumption would represent a saving of 1 billion ECU per year.

While some more recent buildings in central and eastern Europe have better thermal performance, in general the energy consumption, in terms of delivered energy, for heating residential buildings is two to three times higher than similar buildings in western Europe;* typically:

Central and eastern Europe	250-400 kWh/m^2
OECD countries	150-230 kWh/m^2
Scandinavia	120-150 kWh/m^2
'Low energy' housing	60-80 kWh/m^2

* Source: 'Insulation Measures for Retrofitting of Residentail Buildings', 1994, a THERMIE Maxibrochure prepared by Friedemann & Johnson Consultants GmbH - OPET, Berlin for the European Commission Directorate General XVII.

If a building is to be renovated due to deterioration, it is reasonable to combine improvement measures with energy saving ones and to consider the potential for architectural changes, better comfort levels and greater amenity to enhance living conditions and to increase the life span of the building.

BACKGROUND AND OBJECTIVES

The primary intentions of the competition were

- To explore the viability of rehabilitating mass housing in response to growing environmental concerns.

- To inspire building designers by encouraging the development of architectural ideas capable of providing radical improvements in the architectural quality, living environment and energy-efficiency of apartment buildings, with particular reference to buildings in central and eastern Europe.

- To promote the use of innovative conservation technologies integrated with passive solar heating, passive cooling and daylighting techniques, as appropriate to local conditions, as a means to achieve high energy efficiency and more comfortable indoor environments both in the competitors' entries and in their future buildings.

- To contribute to the reduction of energy consumption in buildings and the consequent environmental pollution.

INFORMATION FOR COMPETITORS

BRIEF

Competitors were asked to submit *architectural* proposals for the redesign and upgrading of existing multi-family apartment buildings (and complexes of such buildings) erected since 1945. While transforming the architectural quality of the environment, the proposals should have the potential to significantly improve indoor comfort conditions, thermal performance, and the environmental impact of the building(s) concerned. Proposals were to take account of appropriate 'housekeeping' measures, such as insulation, draught and weather sealing and the control of auxiliary (i.e. mechanical / electrical) heating or cooling, and artificial lighting systems, but the primary focus of the competition was an architectural solution.

Competitors were required to provide a realistic estimate of the annual energy savings per m^2 of original gross floor area in terms of heating, cooling and lighting energy; and design solutions should demonstrate an overall awareness of economy and value.

DOCUMENTATION

The documentation was designed to form an information pack

REGISTRATIONS

Country	Architects	Student block	Student individual	Total
European Union				
Austria	18	80	5	103
Belgium	10	20		30
Denmark	5			5
Finland	5	40		45
France	112	140	16	268
Germany	38	160	11	209
Greece	28	40		68
Ireland	15		3	18
Italy	83	80	22	185
Luxembourg	1			1
Netherlands	18	20	1	39
Portugal	5	40	1	46
Spain	16	20		36
Sweden	10	20	2	32
United Kingdom	46	180	7	233
	410	**840**	**68**	**1318**
EEA				
Norway	1			1
Former Soviet Union				
Armenia	2	20		22
Belarus		20		20
Georgia	1		1	2
Moldova	1			1
Russian Federation	8	140		148
Ukraine			1	1
	12	**180**	**2**	**194**
PECO				
Albania	2		1	3
Bulgaria	2	20		22
Czech Republic	1			1
Estonia	3			3
Hungary	4	40		44
Latvia	1			1
Lithuania	2		1	3
Poland	7	80	2	89
Slovak Republic	5	40		45
Slovenia	6	40		46
	33	**220**	**4**	**257**
TOTAL	**456**	**1,240**	**74**	**1,770**

which was provided to all those who registered. This included design guidelines on passive solar heating, passive cooling and daylighting in a series of wallcharts.

The LT4 Method in booklet form provided data for each relevant climatic region together with related worksheets. These worksheets were used to provide a preliminary indication of the energy performance of the proposed building before and after refurbishment.

Information on four sites (in Berlin, Bourgas, Moscow and Pécs) was provided, although competitors could select an alternative site if so desired.

Documentation was provided in four languages: English, French, German and Russian.

PARTICIPATION

REGISTRATIONS

The period for registration for the competition was from December 1994 to 30 April 1995. A total of 1,770 architects and students registered. Of these registrants, 456 were architects and 1,314 were students.

ENTRIES

SUBMISSION REQUIREMENTS

Competitors were required to submit their designs anonymously on up to four A2 (420 x 594 mm) size sheets in horizontal format. Presentations were to include site plan at a scale 1:500, plans, sections and elevations at scale of 1:200 and other drawings suffcient to explain the design.

Competitors were also asked to submit calculations which indicate the energy performance of the building before and after modification on worksheets contained within the LT4 Method booklet, together with a report on their design.

TECHNICAL ASSESSMENT

An internation panel of fifteen Assessors, including architects, engineers and building physicists, was appointed to advise the Jury on the technical merit of the entries with respect to thermal performance, indoor comfort, environmental impact, technical innovation, potential for replication and economic considerations (see separate Technical Assessors' Report). The Technical Assessors, who met in Dublin on 6 to 8 September 1995 under the joint chairmanship of Nick Baker and Poul Kristensen to conduct the first stage of the competition assessment, were: Nick Baker, Cambridge, United Kingdom; Costas Balaras, Athens, Greece; Elena Bazhenova, Moscow, Russian Federation; Martin de Witt, Eindhoven, The Netherlands; Eric Durand, Vendome, France; Bob Everett, Cambridge, United Kingdom; Paola Fragnito, Milan, Italy; Andreas Hänel, Munich, Germany; Poul Kristensen, Copen-

ENTRIES

Country	Architects	Students	Total
European Union			
Austria	3	4	7
Belgium	2		2
Denmark	1		1
Finland	3	3	6
France	32	13	45
Germany	9	29	38
Greece	1	13	14
Ireland	4		4
Italy	35	4	39
Luxembourg	1		1
Netherlands	4	1	5
Portugal		1	1
Spain	3	4	7
Sweden	4		4
United Kingdom	9	3	12
	111	**75**	**186**
Former Soviet Union			
Armenia	2	2	4
Georgia	1		1
Russian Federation	8	8	16
Ukraine		1	1
	11	**11**	**22**
PECO			
Albania	2		2
Bulgaria	2	3	5
Czech Republic	1		1
Estonia	1		1
Hungary	2	5	7
Latvia	1		1
Lithuania	2	1	3
Poland	2	14	16
Slovak Republic	2	10	12
Slovenia	2	6	8
	17	**39**	**56**
TOTAL	**139**	**125**	**264**

(One entry was disqualified in the architect catagory and two entries were disqualified in the student catagory.)

hagen, Denmark; Paul Leech, Dublin, Ireland; Antonella Marucco, Turin, Italy; Emilio Miguel Mitre, Valladolid, Spain; Simon O'Brien, Dublin, Ireland; Koen Steemers, Cambridge, United Kingdom; János Szász, Pécs, Hungary.

PROCEDURES

The technical assessment – lasting three full days and involving over 370 man-hours – was carried out in two stages:

Initial assessments, by five assessors working individually, produced five separate reports on each entry with grades which were then entered into a computer for analysis. Criteria used at this stage of assessment were:

- Will the design lead to significant improvement in energy efficiency?
- Will it improve the internal environment and/or external environment?
- Is the design technically plausible?
- Does it show a clearly communicated strategy, and is this integrated with architectural issues?
- Is there evidence of quantitative support (e.g. use of the LT Method)?

Based on the grades achieved in the initial assessment, a second-stage assessment was carried out on the more technically proficient entries by two assessors working together for up to one hour per entry. The criteria used at this stage of assessment were:

- Analysis of problem, development and communication of energy / environmental strategy
- Winter heating: fabric, systems and controls
- Summer comfort: shading, ventilation and cooling
- Environmental quality
  internal – daylighting, air quality, acoustic;
  external – site planning, landscaping, microclimate;
  general – use of low-embodied energy/sustainable building materials
- Use of quantitative analysis to support proposal (e.g. LT Method); and improvement in energy efficiency
- Improvement in living conditions and social spaces (indoor and outdoor)
- Potential for replication; and economic considerations

ADJUDICATION

COMPOSITION OF THE JURY

The Jury members for the competition were: Henri Ciriani, Paris; Thomas Herzog, Munich; Jan Kaplicky, London; Henning Larsen, Copenhagen; Alexandros Tombazis, Athens.

ADJUDICATION

Adjudication by the above panel of judges took place in Dublin on 8 to 10 September 1995. Present to assist the Jury were Nick Baker and Poul Kristensen, joint chairmen of the Techni-

cal Assessment panel, who had previously evaluated the projects from the technical point of view (see also Jury's Report).

PRIZE-GIVING

The official announcement of results took place at a prize-giving ceremony on 13 November 1995 at the School of Architecture, University College Dublin.

Prizes and certificates of commendation were awarded by Paul Gormley, Irish Representation European Commission, and the ceremony and exhibition were attended by prize-winners; representatives of University College Dublin, the architectural profession in Ireland, architectural journals; and the public.

DISSEMINATION OF RESULTS

PRESS RELEASE

Results of the competition have been disseminated to journals throughout participating countries and to the UIA for dissemination within their organisation.

EXHIBITIONS

An exhibition of all entries to the competition was held at the School of Architecture, University College Dublin from the 13 to 20 November 1995.

An exhibition of prize-winning and selected schemes was held in the Moscow Union of Architects on 28 to 29 November 1995 and in the Moscow Architectural Institute on the 30 to 31 November 1995.

Further exhibitions are planned for 1996.

CONCLUSION

In conclusion, I would like to thank all the people who have contributed to the organisation of the various stages of the competition and the preparation of the competition documents, in particular to my colleague Vivienne Brophy; Dr Georges Deschamps of DG XII at the Commission for his support; the Judges; the Technical Assessors; the competition Advisory Group; and all of the competitors for their efforts in responding to the many requirements of the brief and contributing to a very sucessful competition.

JOHN GOULDING
Competition Registrar

JURY'S REPORT

There were 261 entries to the competition, 123 from students and 138 from architects. We studied all of the entries with the benefit of the thorough procedure of technical assessment carried out in advance by the panel of 15 technical assessors, and bearing in mind the objectives of the competition which are listed here again, as a reminder:

- To explore the viability of rehabilitating mass housing in response to growing environmental concerns.

- To inspire building designers by encouraging the development of architectural ideas capable of providing radical improvements in the architectural quality, living environment and energy efficiency of apartment buildings, with particular reference to buildings in central and eastern Europe.

- To promote the use of innovative conservation technologies integrated with passive solar heating, passive cooling and daylighting techniques, as appropriate to local conditions, as a means to achieve high energy-efficiency and more comfortable indoor environments both in the competitors' entries and in their future buildings.

- To contribute to the reduction of energy consumption in buildings and the consequent environmental pollution.

It is evident, from the extensive scope of the competition documentation and the large number of sets of documentation distributed to those who registered, that the third and fourth objectives have been achieved.

It was a complex task for competitors to integrate in their designs the many issues of the competition, including aesthetics, energy-efficiency, comfort, economy, applicability, and appropriate use of materials. However, in judging the entries, it became clear that competitors had difficulty in successfully combining these issues. No entry solved all of the conditions satisfactorily; some emphasised energy and environmental aspects while others concentrated on predominantly architectural solutions.

Nonetheless, it can be said that the first and second objectives of the competition were achieved when the range of technical and aesthetic solutions contained in the large number of entries is seen as a resource for the improvement of potentially millions of apartment buildings throughout eastern and western Europe.

The standard of student entries was comparatively high in architectural and technical content, and in both architect and student sections there was a significant level of entries from eastern European countries.

The degree of intervention proposed in each entry had to be interpreted by the Jury in terms of its appropriateness to the conditions of the site location. Therefore, some of the prize-winning projects have received credit for their realism and replicability rather than their architectural or technical glamour. The level of innovation applied mainly to the ingenuity with which known techniques were incorporated in the architectural designs, rather than any development of technical systems.

Few entries gave strong consideration to the improvement of the microclimate or made interventions of quality, strength and persistence in the design of outdoor spaces, integrating them with the architecture of the buildings. The incorporation of environmentally sound materials was also given little attention by most competitors.

Several categories of response have been identified:

- Minimal intervention – simple improvements of the building envelope (insulation, improved glazing), which emphasised economy and value.
- Significant demolition of the existing building and major reconstruction. This approach found little favour among the Jury members due to the high costs involved and because, in essence, it defeated the purpose of the competition.
- Elements added to the building skin – such as sun-spaces and atria, with differing architectural interest from case to case.
- 'Parallel' constructions, which proposed additional accommodation (often including vertical circulation) added to the existing layout.
- Cocoons enveloping the existing building, a strategy which also found little support among the Jury.

In such a complex task as this competition, it seems that it is very difficult to develop a single solution which fully satisfies all of the criteria, and this view is reflected in the prizes awarded. The applicability of some individual designs may be problematic, but the many architectural and technical solutions contained in the body of entries, taken as a whole, may still be seen as an inspiration to architects responsible for the remodelling of apartment buildings.

ARCHITECT SECTION

We award the first prize of 10000 ECU to entry No.26A – NOVAE Architectes, Amilcar Dos Santos, Frank Le Bail and Jean-François Perretant, Lyon, France, for their scheme in Mermoz Sud, Lyon, the *Heart and the Skin*.

This project tackled most of the issues in a convincing and comprehensive manner of good architectural quality. It represents a solution of an intermediate level of intervention, but may be rather expensive to build and has limited potential for replication. The treatment of the ventilation ducts is unsatisfactory and does not add to the project. However, the Jury would like to see the project built as an architectural example.

We wish to award the second prize of 8000 ECU to entry No.39A – Sandrine Jourdain and Olivier Molla, Vitry sur Seine, France, for their scheme in Pécs.

The spaces in this elegant, refined scheme have a luminous quality. It offers a considerable amelioration of the internal spaces with excellent spatial integration. Good use has been made of lightweight panels, although the structural interventions could be disputed. The quality and sensitivity of presentation reflect the quality of the design.

The third prize of 6000 ECU is awarded to entry No.102A – Harry Hagan, Helsinki, Finland, for his scheme on the Marzhan site in Berlin.

This is a low-key but elegant project which is well pre-

sented and communicated. It treats a 'heavy' building in a light, fine manner and provides an exemplary solution which does not involve such major destruction of the existing fabric. Account is taken of the life-cycle and durability of construction materials.

A joint fourth prize of 1500 ECU each is awarded to entry No.44A – Félix Jové Sandoval, Valladolid, Spain, for his scheme in Pécs, and entry No.38A – Pierre Drolez and Elisabeth Lemercier, Paris, France, for their scheme on the Marzhan site in Berlin.

Entry No.44A: A prime example of low-key intervention which still achieves a significant level of improvement at modest cost, and has good potential for replication. The design has been executed in a clear and simple manner, but could be improved by further development. The design is very consequent to the written text provided.

Entry No.38A: This project takes a completely opposite approach to the other joint fourth prize winner. It does everything that the other scheme does not do, and taken together, they illustrate two radically different approaches to the same problem. While of significant architectural quality, it is not thoroughly developed in terms of energy and environmental issues.

We commend one entry – entry No.95A – Rob Marsh, Büro-E, Copenhagen, Denmark, for his scheme on the Marzhan site in Berlin.

This project addressed the energy and environmental issues in a convincing manner, and was chosen by the Jury for its sensitive use of materials, its ecological image and good energy performance. The durability of timber on the facade may be problematic, especially at joints.

STUDENT SECTION

We wish to award a first prize of 5000 ECU to entry No.34B – Kai Hansen, Stephanie Heese, Jan Rützel and Anke Stollberg, Technische Universitat, Berlin, Germany, for their scheme on the Marzhan site in Berlin.

This solution places emphasis on the innovative use of a jalousie device on the elevations which is capable of being stored when not needed, and can accommodate both double-glazed units or panels of transparent insulation. Its deployment can be activated by users directly, or can be automated to control solar radiation reaching the building fabric. Its use in controlling acoustic conditions indoors is questionable, and probably is only effective when fully closed. The cost may also be prohibitive. Several small diagrams clearly show the operation of the building under different conditions.

We award the second prize of 4000 ECU to entry No.10B – Kristian Uthe-Spencker and Laurie Baggett, École d'Architecture de Bordeaux, France, for their scheme on La Cité Lumineuse, Bordeaux.

The presentation of this entry has been beautifully executed. Re-thinking of the internal spaces is the main thrust of the proposal, but the treatment of energy issues is also handled convincingly. Considerable effort has been taken to avoid the monotony often associated with such large buildings. The quantity and quality of information provided in this student project is impressive. It is evident from this project and others from the same stable, that the staff in the Bordeaux school have been influential in promoting good bioclimatic design, and should be congratulated.

The third prize of 3000 ECU is awarded to entry No.58B – Petteri Piha, Helsinki University of Technology, Finland, for his scheme in a northern suburb of Helsinki.

This scheme shows a good balance of economy and innovation and is of significant architectural quality. Traditions have been respected in this no-nonsense project which is a good example for Finnish conditions.

The fourth prize of 1000 ECU is awarded to entry No.6B – Eva Förster, Richard Guy and Vincent Andrieu, École d'Architecture de Paris Belleville, France, for their scheme on the Marzhan site in Berlin.

Although this project did not fulfil many of the basic energy issues, it does demonstrate an architectural quality. Even though some issues such as daylighting and ventilation are not fully resolved, there is the intention to resolve these issues. Spaces are divided between served spaces and those which serve. While the project is somewhat deficient in its treatment of energy issues, it does have a redeeming architectural quality.

We wish to commend two entries: entry No.13B – Christiane Fischer and Sabine Heine, École d'Architecture de Bordeaux, France, for their scheme on La Cité Lumineuse, Bordeaux, and entry No.18B – Enrique Larrumbide Gomez-Rubiera, Escuela Technica Superior de Arquitectura de Madrid, Spain, for his scheme in Pécs.

Entry No.13B is commended for its treatment of scale which gives a truly residential 'feel' to the proposal. It has not been as thoroughly developed, in terms of energy and architectural issues, as the other entry from École d'Architecture de Bordeaux, No.10B, but it does demonstrate a good level of communication and presentation of ideas.

Entry No.18B is commended for the simple and sensitive manner in which it transforms the Pécs building on which it is based.

The following schemes were selected by the Jury for special mention:

Architects

5A	Studio E Architects, London, United Kingdom
21A	Héléne Mehats Grutter and Alexander Grutter, Strassbourg, France
55A	Roberto Grio, Rome, Italy
106A	Wojciech Korbel, Cracow, Poland
46A	Judith Ubarrechena, L2M Architects, San Sebastian, Spain
124A	Dimitris Polychronopoulos, Matina Georgopoulou and George Kontoroupis, Athens, Greece
33A	Andrew Holmes, Paris, France
80A	Karel Vandenhende, Gent, Belgium
61A	Prof. Sergio Croce and Prof. Emilio Pizzi, Milan, Italy
36A	Florence Champíot and Isabelle Ducos, Bordeaux, France
91A	Mari Duffner, Frankfurt, Valeria Retamal-Pucheu, Hamburg, Germany
22A	Philippe Lamarque and Pierre Guillot, Bordeaux, France

Students

8B	Ange Leonforte, École d'Architecture Marseille Luminy, France
60B	Samuli Miettinen, Tampere University of Technology, Finland
83B	Milica Buncáková and Stefan Onofrej, Slovak Technical University, Bratislava, Slovakia
88B	Roswitha Kalckstein and Thomas Sigl, Technical University Vienna, Austria
36B	Klaus Abert, Markus Hegner, Carsten Würffel, Fachhochschule Coburg, Germany
110B	Iota Aggelopoulou, Giorgos Atsalakis, Stavroula Christofilopoulou, National Technical University, Athens, Greece
17B	Beatriz Inglés Gosálbez, Alberto Gomez Espinosa, Javier Bernarte Paton, Escuela Técnica Superior de Arquitectura de Madrid, Spain
20B	Susana Rodriguez Garcia, Patricia Pintado Casas, Rafael Gomez Martinez, Escuela Técnica Superior de Arquitectura de Madrid, Spain
30B	Atelier 'Ap-Art', Uta Kleffling, Stefan Paulisch, Ralph Riesmeier, Apolda, Germany
94B	Vladimir Velinov, University of Architecture, Civil Engineering and Geodesy, Sofia, Bulgaria
98B	Marko Peterlin, University of Ljubljana, Slovenia

We would also like to mention some schemes which received excellent marks from the Technical Assessors:

Architects

95A	Rob Marsh, Büro-E, Copenhagen, Denmark
5A	Studio E Architects Ltd.,London, United Kingdom
25A	Delta Architectes SA, Annecy, France
8A	Brian Jones, York, United Kingdom
26A	Novae Architectes, Lyon, France
43A	Martin Mulligan, Junglinster, Luxembourg
79A	Pierre Sauveur, Liege, Belgium
129A	**Мохорев Евгений Дмитриевич, Владимир, Россия**
110A	Henrich Pifko and Peter Matiasovsky, Bratislava, Slovakia

46A   Judith Ubarrechena, L2M Architects, San
       Sebastian, Spain

Students

8B   Ange Leonforte, École d'Architecture Marseille
       Luminy, France
60B   Samuli Miettinen, Tampere University of
       Technology, Finland
86B   Ivan Redi, Andrea Schröttner, Technical
       University Graz, Austria
88B   Roswitha Kalckstein and Thomas Sigl, Technical
       University Vienna, Austria
83B   Milica Buncáková and Stefan Onofrej, Slovak
       Technical University, Bratislava, Slovakia
10B   Kristian Uthe-Spencker and Laurie Baggett,
       École d'Architecture de Bordeaux, France
36B   Klaus Abert, Markus Hegner, Carsten Würffel,
       Fachhochschule Coburg, Germany
3B   Paul Martin Sandford, South Bank University,
       London, United Kingdom

Henri Ciriani

Thomas Herzog

Henning Larsen

Jan Kaplicky

Alexandros Tombazis

In congratulating the winners, we would like to thank all of the entrants for undertaking the very difficult task of producing both architecture and technical innovation, and for setting to it with a will and often considerable elegance in the result. We wish, finally, to congratulate the Energy Research Group, University College Dublin for the smooth and professional running of the competition.

HENRI CIRIANI

THOMAS HERZOG

HENNING LARSEN

JAN KAPLICKY

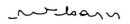

ALEXANDROS TOMBAZIS
(Chairman of the Jury)

TECHNICAL ASSESSORS' REPORT

Unlike the previous competition in this series, the subject of *Living in the City*, the refurbishment and up-grading of existing high rise residential buildings, is highly focused and constrained. We wondered if this would result in a plethora of engineering specifications – applied insulation, weather-stripping, improved boilers, etc, making our task relatively easy, if a little boring. But a cursory glance around the two halls containing a total of 261 entries showed that architectural solutions had been high on the designer's agendas, and even the engineering aspects often showed complexity and creativeness in application. For the technical assessors this is quite demanding, since technical excellence is often implicit in the design rather than explicit and amenable to simple criteria.

Although the entrants were from two groups – practising architects and students, the assessors agreed that there was no significant difference between them in terms of technical design competence. We think that it is encouraging that low energy design is a design issue being addressed by both groups.

To meet these demands and an increased number of entrants, a new procedure was used this year. A first round of assessment selected the top 35% of schemes in a vote where every scheme was briefly reviewed independently by five of the technical experts, referring to a checklist of criteria. The members of the panel were asked to rate the schemes 1 to 4 in descending order of merit. An examination of the scores showed good consistency, with grades rarely differing by more than 1 grade. Where there was wider divergence, these schemes were examined and if scoring at least one grade 1, were included in the next round.

The top 35% were then subjected to closer scrutiny. Assessors worked in pairs and were asked to make detailed comments under a number of topics and to make a short overall report on each scheme. Grading was basically the same but enhanced by + and -. After this assessment, two further assessors briefly reviewed the assessment and approved, or by negotiation moderated, the final mark. This mark was conveyed to the Jury with the recommendation that winners should be selected from grades A or B.

But now to the subject matter itself. The vast majority of entrants had attended to obvious measures such as insulation and reduced infiltration. In some cases unconventional materials such as cork and cellulose fibre had been specified as insulation for their 'green' performance, but it is interesting to note that embodied energy and pollution aspects of materials did not figure as highly as we expected. Not surprisingly, the measures most in evidence were those that had architectural implications and the favourite here was the glazing-in of balconies and in some cases the secondary glazing of whole facades. Provided that suitable shading was included for the more southern locations, the former strategy was considered by the technical assessors to be appropriate. However, most of us had doubts about the secondary glass since this carried much greater environmental problems of overheating, noise, fire, etc, apart from the high cost and technological investment.

Some schemes showed a minimal intervention strategy, focusing in on the most cost-effective way of meeting both the social and energy requirements of the brief. On the other hand, others used the competition to explore many measures and technologies, often within one scheme. In the spirit of an Ideas Competition, this had to be regarded positively. However, the specific topic of high rise residential buildings with many references to social as well as technical problems, did imply some kind of economic restraint.

The best schemes were those which took a more balanced and realistic approach to the expected performance of various systems. In the cold regions of Europe, with very low winter temperatures, the main concern was with insulation and the maximising of solar gains, sometimes employing ventilation pre-heating from a sunspace. Some assistance was given in quantifying these effects by the use of LT4, the energy design tool developed specially for the competition, and it was encouraging to see that almost all of the participants had used this.

The atrium was as popular as ever, carrying with it advantages of a moderated microclimate and reduced conductive and ventilation losses. However, atria in hot climates are difficult to guard from overheating, and often the impact of the structure and shading devices on the views and daylighting of the occupants was not fully considered.

In the warmer climate regions the successful designs included proper provision for shading, ventilation, and the cooling of thermal mass by ventilation at night. Advanced devices such as earth tubes and solar chimneys were less well handled, often (in the opinion of the technical assessors), having fundamental design errors or being incorrectly sized. In some schemes, however, overheating had not been considered adequately even in cases when the use of the LT overheating procedures showed that the building did not reach the accepted criterion.

It was encouraging to see that some participants had responded to the recommendation of the brief to attend to landscaping, both from a social and physical environmental viewpoint.

The overall impression was that the schemes showed there was a widespread awareness of passive and low energy design, and that this could, in many cases, be applied appropriately to existing buildings, a far more important target than new buildings. However, it has to be said that the level of detailed technical knowledge was generally not good; there were few schemes that could be developed to realisable projects without major design development, and many were fundamentally flawed. This illustrates the continued need for design support and technical dissemination if we are to see significant contribution to reducing the environmental impact of energy use in the building sector.

After the technical assessment which took fifteen experts three full days, the two co-chairmen stayed on to brief the Jury and to help with any technical queries which arose. There was good correlation between schemes selected in the first round of technical evaluation and those selected by the architectural judges in the first round.

Only one prizewinner was selected who had not been included in the top 35% in the first technical selection. However, there was less correlation between the detailed technical assessment and final prize-winners. Perhaps this was in part due to the nature of the topic – an *ideas* competition with all the creative freedom that that implies, applied to a very pragmatic and down-to earth problem of improving large residential blocks, often in socially and economically deprived areas. Where on this spectrum should they be judged?

The result is that although there is an underlying technical theme to this competition, some schemes have been judged on their architectural merits rather than their technical excellence. The degree to which these two aspects are separable, will no doubt, continue to be debated.

Finally, on a more positive note, the technical assessors (half of whom were themselves architects) enjoyed viewing a wealth of creative design, from both viewpoints and felt that they had learned much from the experience.

NICK BAKER

POUL KRISTENSEN

DESIGN TOOLS

BRIEF AND CONDITIONS

INTRODUCTION

An architectural ideas competition is announced for the remodelling and upgrading of multi-family apartment buildings constructed in the past five decades in Europe and for the innovative application of conservation technologies using passive solar heating, passive cooling and daylighting. The competition is sponsored by the European Commission, Directorate General XII for Science Research and Development (hereinafter referred to as the promoter). The competition is open to all architects and architectural students resident within the European Union, the European Free Trade Area, and the new democracies of central and eastern Europe.

After the Second World War, many European countries faced an acute housing problem. The requirements of short construction times, low costs and industrialised production led to mass-construction of pre-fabricated concrete buildings. Unrealistically low energy prices and lack of appropriate materials has, in some regions, often resulted in buildings with low levels of thermal insulation, inadequate means of regulating comfort levels and little individual metering or billing of energy consumption, leading to very high energy use in buildings.

About 40% of total energy consumption in Europe is used in buildings, many of which are large apartment buildings made of pre-fabricated components. Large numbers are in need of major renovation due to poor construction quality or deterioration with age, and the potential for energy savings is huge. If energy saving measures are combined with general renovation to improve amenity, then costs and pay-back periods can be reduced significantly.

Between 1945 and 1975 approximately ten million apartment units were constructed in the European Community as it was then. If a figure of 500 ECU is taken as the average annual energy cost for each apartment, then a relatively modest reduction of 20% in energy consumption would represent a saving of 1 billion ECU per year.

Some more recent buildings in central and eastern Europe have better thermal performance, but in general, the energy consumption, in terms of delivered energy, for heating residential buildings is two to thee times higher than similar buildings in western Europe; typically:

Central and eastern Europe	250-400 kWh/m^2
OECD countries	150-230 kWh/m^2
Scandinavia	120-150 kWh/m^2
'Low energy' housing	60-80 kWh/m^2

Source: 'Insulation Measures for Retrofitting of Residentail Buildings', 1994, a THERMIE 'Maxibrochure' prepared by Friedemann & Johnson Consultants GmbH – OPET, Berlin for the European Commission Directorate General XVII

If a building is to be renovated due to deterioration, it is reasonable to combine improvement measures with energy saving ones and to consider the potential for architectural changes, better comfort levels and greater amenity to enhance living conditions and to increase the life span of the building.

The design should consider, as a fundamental issue, improvements to the design of the individual apartments and adjacent spaces (balconies, hallways etc.).

OBJECTIVES

The primary intentions of the competition are:

- To explore the viability of rehabilitating mass housing in response to growing environmental concerns.

- To inspire building designers by encouraging the development of architectural ideas capable of providing radical improvements in the architectural quality, living environment and energy- efficiency of apartment buildings, with particular reference to buildings in central and eastern Europe.

- To promote the use of innovative conservation technologies integrated with passive solar heating, passive cooling and daylighting techniques, as appropriate to local conditions, as a means to achieve high energy-efficiency and more comfortable indoor environments both in the competitors' entries and in their future buildings.

- To contribute to the reduction of energy consumption in buildings and the consequent environmental pollution.

BACKGROUND

Four previous competitions promoted by the European Commission during the past ten years have addressed the application of passive solar design in buildings. The first two focused on residential buildings. The third competition, *Working in the City*, sought to emphasise the application of these principles in non-domestic buildings, with particular attention to daylighting. The fourth EC architectural ideas competition, entitled *Zephyr*, focused on passive cooling of mixed-use (residential and commercial) buildings in the Mediterranean region.

This latest competition, *Living in the City*, seeks to stimulate the development of architectural solutions which address the problems of general amenity, comfort and poor thermal performance associated with many of the multi-family apartment buildings erected since the Second World War. The competition will relate particularly to buildings and complexes of buildings in central and eastern Europe, but will have relevance to apartment buildings throughout Europe.

The competition will encourage the exploration of new concepts, innovative products and more radical approaches to this great challenge, while creating employment and business opportunities.

Given the slow rate of replacement of Europe's residential building stock, the redesign and upgrading of existing buildings can contribute significantly to a reduction in energy consumption and global environmental pollution. Moreover, the very real opportunities for energy savings which exist within the EU Member States are small when compared with the potential in the new democracies of central and eastern Europe, where the issue of the rehabilitation or reconstruction of mass housing is a growing priority.

Although having special relevance in central and eastern Europe, this competition offers stimulating opportunities and a challenge to the architectural profession and schools of architecture throughout the continent.

GENERAL CONDITIONS

The competition is an international, single stage ideas competition open to all architects resident in the European Union, the European Free Trade Area, and the new democracies of central and eastern Europe, and to students of architecture, irrespective of nationality, registered at schools of architecture in these regions.

Architects and students may enter as individuals, or in groups, or may set up multi-disciplinary teams and/or transnational teams for the purposes of entering this competition. Based on the experience of previous, similar competitions, the involvement of a building physicist or a building services engineer in the design team may have a significant effect on the technical quality of the design.

Where entries describe actual projects intended for realisation, construction work shall not have commenced before 31 March 1995, the opening date for this competition.

The official languages of the competition are English, French, German and Russian.

The competition has been approved by the International Union of Architects.

BRIEF

The competition seeks architectural proposals for the redesign and upgrading of existing multi-family apartment buildings (and complexes of such buildings) erected since 1945. While transforming the architectural quality of the environment, the proposals should have the potential to significantly improve indoor comfort conditions, thermal performance, and the environmental impact of the building(s) concerned. Proposals should take account of appropriate 'housekeeping' measures, such as insulation, draught and weather sealing and the control of auxiliary (i.e. mechanical / electrical) heating or cooling, and artificial lighting systems, but the primary focus of the competition is an architectural solution.

Proposals may relate to an individual apartment building or to groups of such buildings.

Proposals should show responses to the needs and opportunities for energy-efficient heating, cooling and daylighting which are appropriate to the required comfort levels, the chosen site, climate, urban context and building(s).

Competitors will be required to provide a realistic estimate of the annual energy savings per m^2 of original gross floor area in terms of heating, cooling and lighting energy.

The site for the proposed building may be one of those described in the accompanying package entitled 'Useful Background Information'. Alternatively, competitors may select another site, located within the regions indicated on the climatic zones map.

Design solutions should demonstrate an overall awareness of economy and value.

Competitors are required to set their own detailed brief. As an indication, the gross floor area of the building(s) should be not less than $450m^2$

CRITICAL DATES

Last date for registration	30 April 1995
Closing date for entries	31 July 1995 at 17.30 hrs GMT
Adjudication by international jury	September 1995
Announcement of results	October 1995

JURY

– Henri Ciriani, Paris
– Thomas Herzog, Munich
– Jan Kaplicky, London,
– Henning Larsen, Copenhagen
– Alvaro Siza, Porto
– Alexandros Tombazis, Athens

A number of expert assessors will be appointed to help the jury by assessing technical aspects of the design proposals.

In the event of the inability of any juror to act, through illness or other cause, another shall be appointed in his or her place by the promoter.

AWARDS

Prizes will be awarded to the designs that the jury considers to represent the most innovative responses to the challenges set out in the objectives and brief:

Section 1: ARCHITECTS	First prize	15000 ECU
	Second prize	7000 ECU
	Third prize	3500 ECU
	Fourth prize	1500 ECU
Section 2: STUDENTS	First Prize	7000 ECU
	Second prize	3000 ECU
	Third prize	2000 ECU
	Fourth prize	1000 ECU

A further number of schemes may be selected to receive commendations.

The distribution of the prize fund may be varied at the discretion of the Jury.

The promoter undertakes to accept the decisions of the Jury and to pay the prizes within one month of the announcement of awards.

REGISTRATION

The registrar for the competition, to whom all entries should be addressed, is:
John Goulding, Energy Research Group, University College Dublin, Richview, Clonskeagh, IRL-Dublin 14.

The following documents will be issued to registered competitors:
- Competition Conditions and Procedures
- An envelope containing 'Useful Background Information' on passive solar heating, passive cooling, daylighting and urban design guidelines, and descriptions of the optional or 'default' sites
- The LT4 Method – in booklet form (including data for each relevant climatic region) together with related worksheets.
- Entry / Declaration Form, Declaration Envelope, and Pre-Addressed Label

A book of the competition results, containing all prize-winning and commended entries, will be published. Each registered competitor and group of students will receive a complimentary copy of this book.

SUBMISSION PROCEDURE

Competitors shall present their designs anonymously on up to four A2 (420 mm x 594 mm) size sheets in horizontal format, mounted on lightweight board or card with clear annotation in any of the official languages of the competition, but preferably in English, such that the drawing would remain legible if the A2 sheet were to be reduced to A6. A minimum lettering size of 24 point, bold or medium capitals is recommended for all titles. Drawn scales should be provided where relevant. Colour may be used on the drawings. Entries which are pre-

sented on any other material, such as wood, metal, or glass will be disqualified.

The presentations shall include at least the following information:
- A key map showing the country and indicating the location and latitude of the town or city;
- A site plan at scale 1:500, with the north point and an indication of features which affect the local environment such as overshadowing, prevailing winds or traffic noise;
- Plans, sections and elevations sufficient to explain the design, at scale 1:200 or larger;
- Competitors shall also submit a limited number of specified calculations which indicate the energy performance of the proposed design, and of the building(s) before any modification. The worksheets on which the completed calculations should be entered form part of the competition documentation and are contained in the LT4 Method booklet; competitors shall submit their calculations on photocopies of the worksheets. Competitors are strongly advised to carry out trial calculations to familiarise themselves with the LT4 Method before using it for their competition entry. It is an easy-to-use method which can significantly improve the energy-efficiency of the design if used iteratively during the design process to inform design decisions.
- Models may not be submitted, but photographs of study models should be included as part of the presentation.
- Competitors must submit a typewritten description of the design (maximum two A4 sheets) in any of the official languages of the competition, but preferably in English. This should describe:
  – the essential features of the scheme and its operation under different seasonal and diurnal conditions;
  – relevant aspects of the site and surrounding features; microclimate and chosen building;
  – the passive systems adopted – in order of priority
  – the design strategy adopted and the reasons for doing so;
  – a short statement describing economic conditions in the region which may have a bearing on the economic viability of the proposal.
- Detail Plans, sections and elevations at scale 1:50;
- Diagrammatic representation of the seasonal & diurnal environmental functioning of the building.
- Details of proposed constructional changes at an appropriate scale.

The entry of each competitor shall be contained in a single package which shall be sent, carriage paid or delivered, to the registrar using the pre-addressed label issued with the conditions. Entries shall be submitted without name, motto or any kind of distinguishing mark and shall be accompanied by the entry / declaration of authorship form signed by the competitor(s) and properly sealed in the official envelope.

On receipt of each entry the registrar will allocate a number to each set of panels and to the corresponding envelope. The anonymity of each competitor will be maintained until the adjudication has taken place.

Entries by students arising from block registration shall be individually submitted, using the pre-addressed labels (endorsed STUDENT ENTRY) issued with these conditions, and shall each be accompanied by a signed official entry form properly sealed in an official envelope.

A successful competitor must be prepared to satisfy the assessors that he or she is the bona fide author of the design submitted.

Competitors should retain copies of the designs submitted. The entries, or any other material submitted will not be returned.

RULES

The Jury's decision will be final on all matters regarding this competition. No questions may be asked directly or indirectly, and no correspondence can be entered into.

The competition conditions will be issued in English, French, German, and Russian. In all matters of interpretation, the English language version will take precedence.

Entries are accepted on the basis that they may be published by the sponsors if so required.

A design shall be excluded from the competition for any of the following reasons:
- If received after the latest time for submissions: 17.30 hours GMT on 31 July 1995;
- If, in the opinion of the Jury, any of the conditions other than those of a discretionary nature has been disregarded;
- If a competitor in any way discloses his or her identity, or attempts improperly to influence the decision of the Jury;
- If the entry is made by a Jury member or technical assessor or by a partner, employee, collaborator, spouse or blood relation of any of the Jury members or technical assessors;
- If the entry is made by an employee of the European Commission or the Energy Research Group, University College Dublin.

EXHIBITION AND PUBLICATION

Before the public announcement of the results of the competition is made, all winners will be notified.

All designs submitted will be publicly exhibited in a European capital with the names of the authors attached thereto for a period of not less than six days. Prize winning projects will be exhibited in a number of European venues. The exhibition of selected designs may be made available to interested schools of architecture, professional and other institutes. Enquiries should be addressed to the registrar.

Prize-winning entrants may be invited to make scale models of their designs, in which case a separate budget will be made available. Selected designs will be exhibited at venues to be announced.

A book of the competition results, containing all prize-winning and commended entries, will be published. Each registered competitor and group of students will receive a complimentary copy of this book. It is anticipated that the winning entries will be widely publicised to European architectural periodicals and other media.

COPYRIGHT

The ownership of the copyright of the work of all competitors shall remain the property of the competitors. The promoter retains the right to exhibit and reproduce, without payment but with acknowledgement, any of the entries, in part or full, either separately or together with other entries, with or without explanatory text, within any publication or publicity related to this competition.

PROCEDURES AND REQUIREMENTS
FOR THE COMPETITION

The competition *Living in the City* has as its objective to encourage the production of good urban architecture, and to encourage architects to adopt innovative design strategies appropriate to the climatic context. An important criterion for the competition is that the designs demonstrate the reduction of energy consumption, while improving environmental comfort standards.

The envelope containing 'Useful Background Information' contains information to assist competitors in the development of strategies for heating, cooling, daylighting and urban design, with reference to energy conservation and comfort conditions.

It is important that competitors read this documentation carefully.

The LT4 Method is a graphical aid which gives a preliminary indication of the overall energy performance of the building at an early proposal stage. The procedure combines the thermal effect of solar gains and useful daylighting as a function of glazing area and orientation. Competitors are required to fill in and submit a photocopy of the worksheet contained in this section. Evidence of competitors' use of the design tool LT4 will form a significant part of the technical assessment which will be communicated to the jury. It is intended to be used iteratively as the design progresses, so that the effects of design changes on energy consumption can be seen.

The LT4 Method 4.0

An Energy Design Tool for the Refurbishment of Residential Buildings

1   INTRODUCTION

The mechanism of energy use in buildings is complex, involving three main factors; the physical building itself, the efficiency of the energy-using equipment such as heating plant and lighting, and the way that the occupants control the building and systems. Different combinations of these factors lead to a wide variance in energy use. For example, poor fabric insulation, an inefficient boiler, and occupants controlling excess heat by opening windows, will all contribute to very high energy use.

Refurbishment provides the opportunity to directly improve the building fabric and the systems, and these improvements may promote better occupant performance. For example, the fitting of room thermostats would remove the need for occupants to open windows to control overheating in winter.

In developing a strategy, it is useful to be able to rank the impact of various measures. Savings are not simply additive – for example the value of heating energy saved by applying insulation would be greater for a district heating system of inherently low efficiency, than it would be for a building with its own high efficiency boiler.

2   THE LT METHOD 4

The LT Method 4 is a design tool for use when establishing a strategy for energy conservation. Earlier versions of the LT Method have considered energy for artificial lighting, heating, cooling and ventilation (hence the name LT, standing for Lighting and Thermal) in non-residential buildings. In residential buildings, energy use is dominated by heating and so this version of LT only predicts heating energy in detail. Although not directly related to energy use, summer comfort is of great importance. LT4 includes a simple overheating risk indicator.

It is important to note that the LT Method is an approximate method only, to be used for establishing orders of priority and rough indications of cost effectiveness. It is not a precision method which could be used to predict the energy use of an actual building; its main value is for making comparisons between various refurbishment options.

The LT Method 4 responds to the following:
1.   Climate
2.   Building form and size
3.   Thermal conductance of walls and roof
4.   Area and distribution of glazing
5.   Type of glazing (single, double, triple or low-E)
6.   Air infiltration rate
7.   Presence of sunspace or atrium.
8.   Heating system efficiency

Clearly the first two factors are given constraints. The remaining ones all provide possible subjects for improvement as part of refurbishment.

LT4 is a manual method. By means of pre-calculated

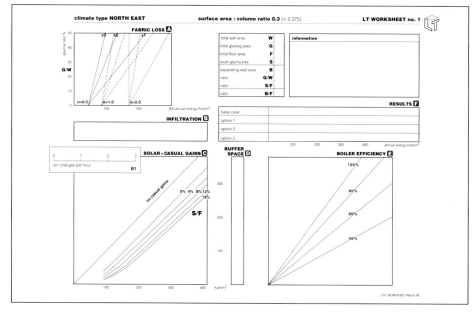

Figure 1
LT Worksheet

Figure 2
Approximate LT4 climate zones

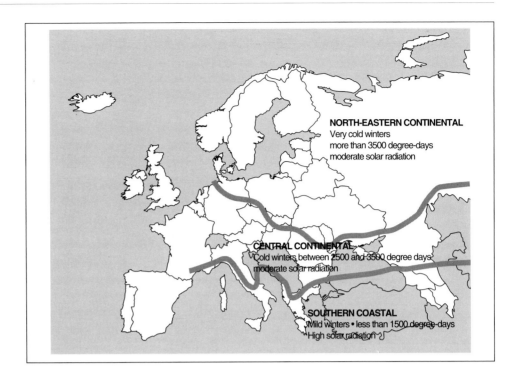

NORTH-EASTERN CONTINENTAL
Very cold winters
more than 3500 degree-days
moderate solar radiation

CENTRAL CONTINENTAL
Cold winters between 2500 and 3500 degree days
moderate solar radiation

SOUTHERN COASTAL
Mild winters • less than 1500 degree-days
High solar radiation

graphs the user performs a sequence of estimations as follows:
1. Fabric heat loss
2. Infiltration heat loss
3. Savings from solar and internal gains
4. Effect of sunspace
5. Effect of heating plant efficiency.

LT 4 has an output in the form of annual energy use per square metre floor area. This is to allow comparison between the building under consideration and target values which are independent of the building size. Clearly it is a simple matter to convert this output to a total energy consumption value for a particular building by multiplying by the total floor area. The graphs are presented as a worksheet, which can be photocopied, drawn and written upon to form a record of the options compared. The LT 4 Worksheet is illustrated in Figure 1, and detailed instructions for use are given on page 28.

3 CLIMATE

Heating energy is influenced primarily by winter temperatures, represented by heating degree-days, and secondarily by the availability of solar radiation. These two climatic variables are used to characterise three climate zones. Figure 2 shows these zones on the map of Europe. This is approximate only and the choice of the appropriate LT zone should be made by reference to the degree-day data given. At heights of more than 750 m above sea level, when using the map to define the zone, the next colder zone should be selected. This particularly applies to the mountainous areas in the continental southern zone. These zones are defined primarily for winter heating calculation; the procedure for estimating summer overheating uses zones defined in a different way, in the LT Overheating Predictor section.

4 BUILDING FORM AND ORIENTATION

The energy consumption per square metre is dependent upon the ratio of envelope surface area to building volume, or (since floor-to-ceiling heights are relatively uniform) surface area to floor area. This ratio will vary for a tall narrow tower and a deep slab. It will also become greater (and therefore have greater heat loss) for smaller buildings. LT charts have been produced for only three ranges of this parameter in order to keep the number of charts to a manageable number.

However, energy consumption is quite sensitive to this ratio. If a final energy figure is required to compare with other buildings, or energy targets, and the surface area to volume ratio is not close to one of the three values, then two charts should be used and the final value obtained by interpolation.

Orientation of the building influences the distribution of glazing with respect to south, the direction from which most useful solar gains will be made in winter.

5 CONDUCTIVE LOSSES

The conductive losses are controlled primarily by the thermal conductance of the opaque wall and roof, the thermal conductance of the glazing, and the glazing ratio - the ratio of the area of glass to the total wall area (including the glass and framing). Since the conductance (U-value) of glass is generally much greater than that of opaque wall, the glazing ratio is critical in determining the overall conductive heat loss. In preparing the LT graphs it is assumed that the roof U-value (conductance) is the same as the wall value. However, where they are known to differ by a large amount, and for building forms which have a relatively large roof area, an area-weighted mean U-value could be calculated and used when choosing the appropriate LT curve.

For calculating fabric loss, curves for three levels of wall insulation are provided corresponding to (a) uninsulated, U-value = 2.0 (b) low insulation, U-value = 1.0, and (c) high insulation, U-value = 0.5. It is quite easy to interpolate or extrapolate the curves for other values. Three glazing types are assumed; single glazing U-value = 5.5, double glazing U-value = 3, triple or low-E glazing U-value = 2.

Improved insulation is an important refurbishment option and can be achieved by (a) internal insulation lining (b) external insulation over-cladding, and (c) cavity insulation if a suitable cavity is present. All have advantages and disadvantages; these and practical details are discussed in the Design Guidelines

Cold bridges may increase the average U-value of the wall considerably, particularly in the case when insulation is on the inside surfaces. Information on these factors can be found in the Design Guidelines. However, the increased risk of condensation and mould growth at the sites of cold bridges, is often more important than the extra heat loss.

6   INFILTRATION

Infiltration is the ingress of air from the outside through the fabric, through cracks around windows and doors. Cracks can also exist between components such as door and window frames and the wall in which they are located, and between components such as wall panels, floors, facias and soffits. Infiltration between components is particularly prevalent in pre-fabricated and partially pre-fabricated systems. Infiltration (and intentional ventilation) constitute a heat loss due to the demand for heat to bring the incoming air up to room temperature.

It is generally agreed that for domestic activities ventilation rates of between 0.5 ac/h and 1.0 ac/h are sufficient, the lower values assuming that sources of heavy domestic pollution such as cooking and clothes-drying are ventilated locally. However, in many buildings, even the infiltration through unintentional openings such as the cracks described above, may lead to air change rates as high as 3 ac/h, in winter when the driving forces of wind and temperature difference are at their greatest.

This over-ventilation is wasteful of heating energy, and the reduction of uncontrolled ventilation (infiltration) during the general upgrading of the fabric is a valuable re-furbishment option. It can be achieved by weather stripping of openable doors and windows, re-caulking construction joints, or as part of over-cladding.

Some caution must be exercised however since by lowering overall ventilation rates, some rooms may become under-ventilated. Thus more care must be given to the flow paths from room to room, and as already mentioned, the exhausting of domestic pollutants at source. Estimation of the infiltration rate is assisted by reference to Table 1.

7   SOLAR GAINS

The distribution of the glazing with respect to orientation influences the availability of useful solar gains. The parameter used to estimate this is the ratio of the area of south-facing glazing to the total floor area. Within the accuracy of the method, south-facing can be taken as any glazing facing within 45° of south. Orientation will also be relevant when estimating overheating probability.

The effect of solar gains is estimated using the second

Table 1 – Estimation of Infiltration Rate

EXPOSURE OF BUILDING			
E	low	0.8	
	medium	1.0	
	high	1.3	

CONSTRUCTION				
C	1	pre-cast panel + dry lining	10	
	2	case 1 + plaster	6	
	3	masonary + plaster	2	
	4	case 1 + sealed overcladding	3	

WINDOWS AND DOORS				
D	1	single leaf, bad fitting, deck access no lobby	10	
	2	double window + draughty lobby	6	
	3	case 1 + weatherstripping	6	
	4	case 2 + weatherstripping	4	
	5	high performance, new	2	

To estimate infiltration:

infiltration rate = (C+D) multiplied by (E) divided by (D)

Note – An infiltration rate of less than 0.5 ac/h should not be used. In practice, deliberate ventilation by the occupants should provide this to ensure adequate air quality.

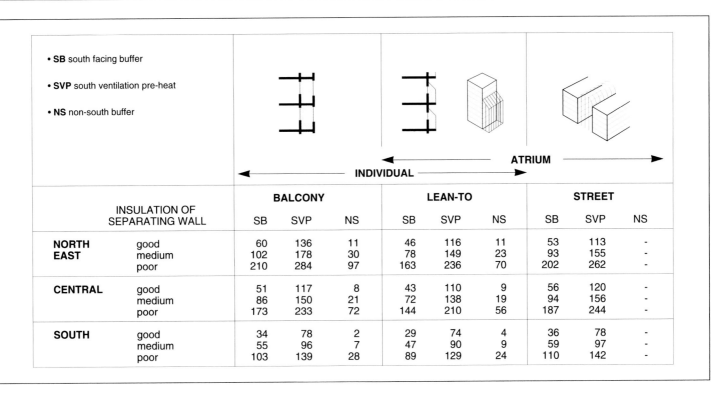

- **SB** south facing buffer
- **SVP** south ventilation pre-heat
- **NS** non-south buffer

INSULATION OF SEPARATING WALL		BALCONY			LEAN-TO			STREET		
		SB	SVP	NS	SB	SVP	NS	SB	SVP	NS
NORTH EAST	good	60	136	11	46	116	11	53	113	-
	medium	102	178	30	78	149	23	93	155	-
	poor	210	284	97	163	236	70	202	262	-
CENTRAL	good	51	117	8	43	110	9	56	120	-
	medium	86	150	21	72	138	19	94	156	-
	poor	173	233	72	144	210	56	187	244	-
SOUTH	good	34	78	2	29	74	4	36	78	-
	medium	55	96	7	47	90	9	59	97	-
	poor	103	139	28	89	129	24	110	142	-

Table 2 – Annual Buffer Space Thermal Savings kWh/m²

LT4 curve. These curves are provided for the particular climate zone and take account of the fraction of solar gain which is useful in displacing auxiliary heating. The curves also include the effect of internal gains from people, lighting and equipment. The presence of thermal mass increases the usefulness of solar gains by storing them and reducing the risk of overheating. The data for the curves is generated by the mathematical model, assuming a medium to heavyweight building construction. In the less common case of a lightweight building, or a building lined with lightweight insulation and lightweight partitions where all the thermal mass is isolated, the solar contribution should be reduced by about 30%. It is also important to note that the solar energy will only reduce auxiliary heating if the control system can respond.

8   SUNSPACES AND ATRIA

Sunspaces and atria (referred to generically as *buffer* spaces) do not have auxiliary heating themselves and reduce heat losses from the spaces to which they are attached by (a) reducing conductive losses through the wall of the heated building, and possibly (b) by providing some ventilation air at a higher temperature than ambient air (often referred to as *ventilation pre-heating*). Both of these effects occur due to heat from the heated building raising the temperature of the unheated buffer spaces, and are further enhanced by solar gains made in the bufferspace. Ventilation pre-heating will only take place if flow paths are designed to encourage airflow from the buffer space to the heated interior.

In LT4 the contribution that the buffer space makes is given in the form of *annual saving per square metre of separating wall*. The separating wall is the area of wall between the heated building and the unheated bufferspace. The saving will also depend on the conductance of the separating wall which is influenced by the level of insulation and the amount of glazing. Values are given for south-facing buffer only, south-facing with ventilation pre-heating, and non-south-facing buffer spaces only.

Three different configurations are identified. The first is where the buffer space is formed by, in effect, glazing over all or part of the south facade to form individual bufferspaces, i.e. there is only south facing vertical glazing. This could be realised by glazing in access galleries or balconies, or providing a 'second skin' of glazing to the facade. The second two cases relate to an atrium configuration, where there is a significant amount of roof glazing. One case is where a large glazed space is attached to the side of a building. The other case is where the space between two buildings is roofed over.

Values of thermal savings are given in Table 2 for the three climate zones.

9   HEATING PLANT EFFICIENCY

The factors discussed above influence the demand for *useful heat*. Two further factors relate this to the amount of energy delivered to the site in the form of fuel: (a) the wastage of heat in its distribution to the point of use (the rooms), and (b) the efficiency with which the fuel is converted into heat. In some cases, residential buildings may be heated by waste heat from power stations (Combined Heat and Power) in which case the efficiency of the initial conversion of fuel to heat becomes less important, provided there is sufficient heat available. System efficiencies can be estimated from Table 3.

To allow inter-comparisons between types of fuel, and to make direct comparisons with electricity use, the final output is in *primary energy*. This is the energy value of the fuel plus the *energy overheads* involved in bringing it to the site and relates well to the cost and to the environmental impact due to CO_2 production and other pollutants.

For most true fuels, the energy overhead is small, but in the case of electricity, for thermodynamic reasons, there is a very large energy overhead when fuel is converted into heat, mechanical and finally electrical power. Typical *delivered to primary energy ratios* for electricity are around 30%. This makes an overwhelming case for *not* using electricity for heating. Even when electricity comes from a renewable source such as windpower or hydro, it can be argued that since Europe has an electricity supply grid, this 'clean' power should be used to displace conventionally generated power.

Table 3 – Annual Heating Plant Efficiencies

		Annual efficiency
1	District or group system, poorly maintained, poorly insulated mains, single pipe emmitters	40%
2	Well maintained district or group system well insulated mains, basic controls	60%
3	Modern lightweight gas or oil boiler, no external mains, room thermostats	80%

10   THE LT WORKSHEET

The worksheet is a series of charts organised so that outputs from one chart can be transferred graphically as an input to the next chart. The steps in using the Worksheet are as follows, using data from the existing building to establish the *base case:*

Start – Select the appropriate worksheet for (a) climate zone and (b) building form, i.e. surface area to volume ratio (For this initial calculation take total surface area to include groundfloor, walls and roof). The Worksheet should then be photocopied.

A few key parameters of the building have to be calculated from the drawings or building description. These are:

W   total external wall area (*excluding* roof and ground floor)
G   total glazing area
F   total floor area (all storeys)
S   south glazing area

These values are used to calculate the ratio **G/W** which is used to calculate the fabric losses, and **S/F** which is used to estimate the solar gains.

If there is a buffer space, the area of separating wall (between the buffer space and the heated building) also has to be specified:

B   separating wall area

This value is used to calculate ratio **B/F** which is used to estimate the energy saving due to the buffer space.

Step A – Enter Chart **A** with the approximate glazing ratio **G/W** on the vertical axis and draw a line across to the appropriate curve. Note that they are grouped into good, medium and poor levels of insulation, each group having curves for single, double, and triple or low-E glazing. If the standard values are unsuitable then interpolate or extrapolate. From the point of intersection transfer the value with a vertical line down to chart **B**. The annual heating energy in KWh/m² (primary energy units) for the conductive losses, is shown where the vertical line crosses the horizontal axis at the bottom of chart **A**.

Step B – By reference to Table 1 or other information use scale B1 to evaluate infiltration heat losses and add this to at the top line of chart **B** by moving horizontally to the right. Interpolate or extrapolate if necessary. Transfer this value with a vertical line down to chart **C**.

Step C – From the value of south glazing area to floor area ratio **S/F**, chose the appropriate curve on chart **C**, or interpolate. If a building has no south-facing glazing, use the 0% curve; this will account for the effect of useful internal gains only. From the point of intersection with the appropriate line transfer the value horizontally to chart **D**.

Step D – If there is a buffer space, determine the *buffer space thermal saving* from Table 2 and deduct from the current energy value in the left hand column of chart **D**, in a similar way to the infiltration energy at chart **B**, but on the vertical axis.

Step E – Determine the heating system efficiency by reference to Table 3 or other sources. Transfer the value from chart **C** or **D** to the appropriate curve. From the point of intersection transfer the value upward to chart **F**.

Step F – Draw the bar chart for the base case. Note that conductive, infiltration and buffer space components could be presented separately as stacked bars. Note also that there is a scale change at chart **E**.

The proposed refurbishment options can now be evaluated in a similar way and there is room for three options to be displayed alongside the base case. The options can be described briefly in the box at the left of the bar chart. A second sheet could be used for further options.

Initially draw on the charts in feint pencil. Then when the chart is completed and confirmed, trace the lines in colour to illustrate the effects of the options.

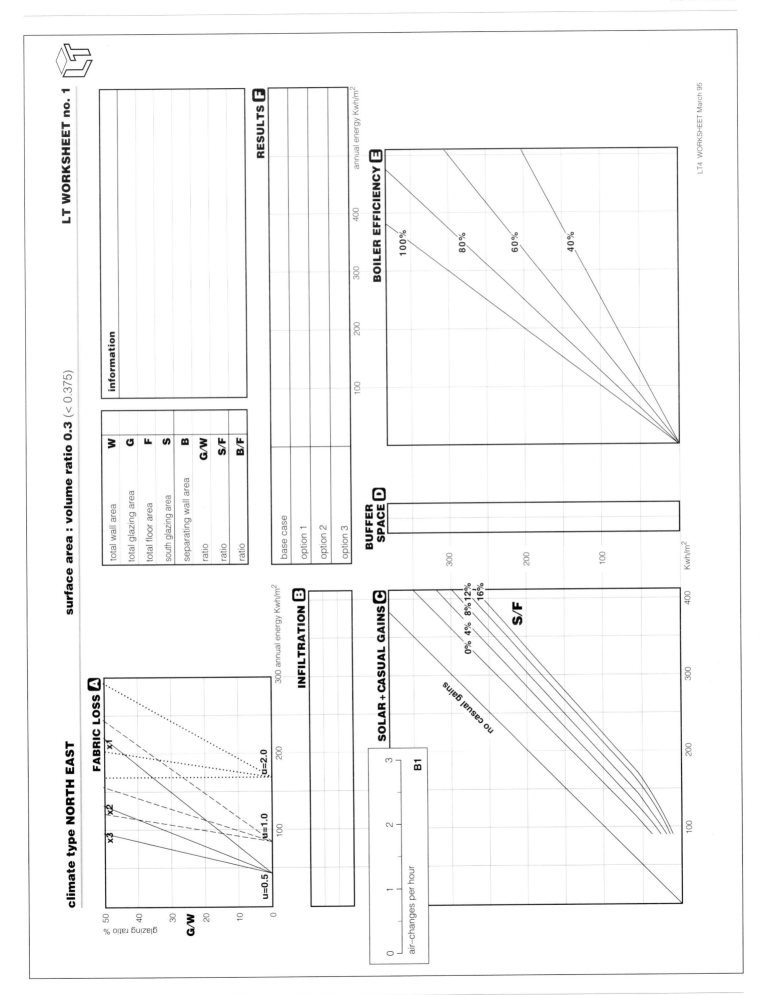

LT4 WORKSHEET March 95

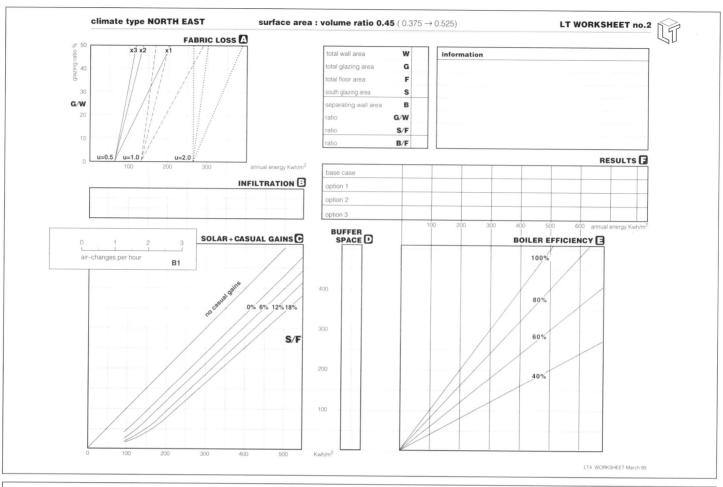

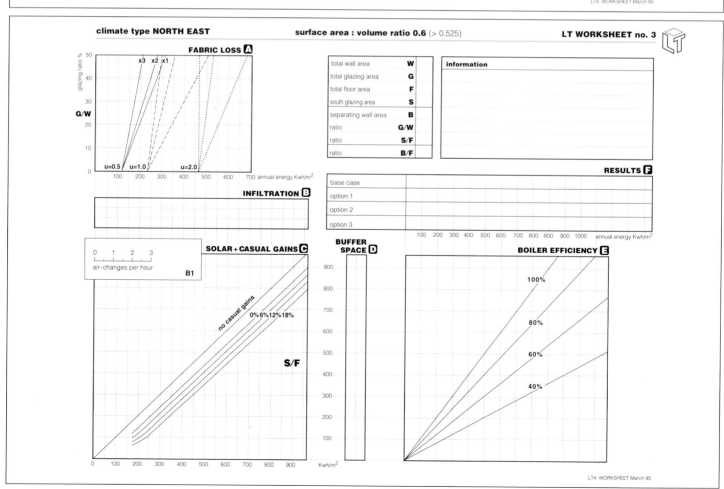

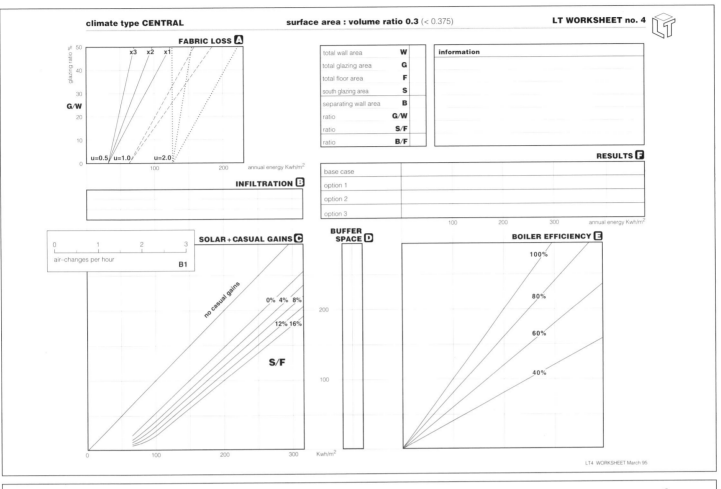

climate type CENTRAL   surface area : volume ratio 0.3 (< 0.375)   LT WORKSHEET no. 4

FABRIC LOSS A

total wall area	W
total glazing area	G
total floor area	F
south glazing area	S
separating wall area	B
ratio	G/W
ratio	S/F
ratio	B/F

information

RESULTS F

| base case |
| option 1 |
| option 2 |
| option 3 |

INFILTRATION B

SOLAR + CASUAL GAINS C

BUFFER SPACE D

BOILER EFFICIENCY E

LT4 WORKSHEET March 95

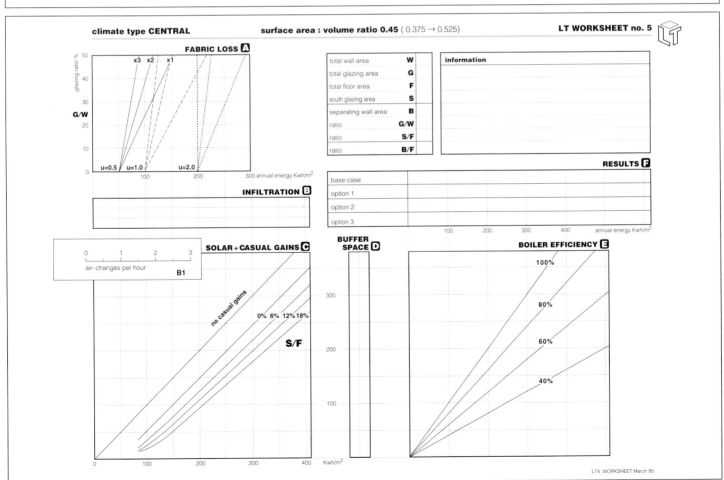

climate type CENTRAL   surface area : volume ratio 0.45 (0.375 → 0.525)   LT WORKSHEET no. 5

FABRIC LOSS A

total wall area	W
total glazing area	G
total floor area	F
south glazing area	S
separating wall area	B
ratio	G/W
ratio	S/F
ratio	B/F

information

RESULTS F

| base case |
| option 1 |
| option 2 |
| option 3 |

INFILTRATION B

SOLAR + CASUAL GAINS C

BUFFER SPACE D

BOILER EFFICIENCY E

LT4 WORKSHEET March 95

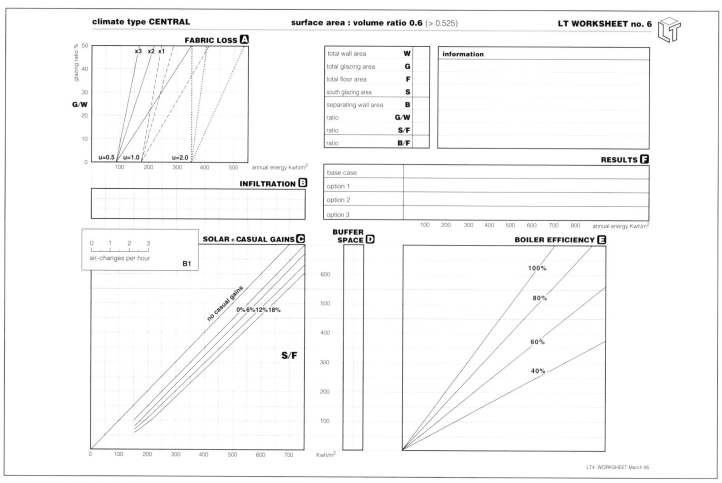

climate type CENTRAL

surface area : volume ratio 0.6 (> 0.525)

LT WORKSHEET no. 6

FABRIC LOSS A

glazing ratio %

G/W

x3 x2 x1

u=0.5 u=1.0 u=2.0

100 200 300 400 500   annual energy Kwh/m²

total wall area	**W**	
total glazing area	**G**	
total floor area	**F**	
south glazing area	**S**	
separating wall area	**B**	
ratio	**G/W**	
ratio	**S/F**	
ratio	**B/F**	

information

RESULTS F

base case	
option 1	
option 2	
option 3	

100 200 300 400 500 600 700 800   annual energy Kwh/m²

INFILTRATION B

0 1 2 3
air–changes per hour

B1

SOLAR + CASUAL GAINS C

no casual gains

0%6%12%18%

S/F

0 100 200 300 400 500 600 700   Kwh/m²

BUFFER SPACE D

600
500
400
300
200
100

BOILER EFFICIENCY E

100%
80%
60%
40%

LT4 WORKSHEET March 95

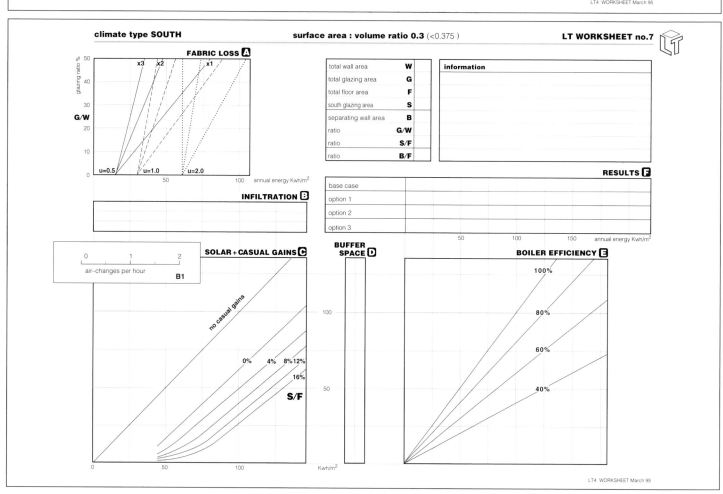

climate type SOUTH

surface area : volume ratio 0.3 (<0.375)

LT WORKSHEET no.7

FABRIC LOSS A

glazing ratio %

G/W

x3 x2 x1

u=0.5 u=1.0 u=2.0

50 100   annual energy Kwh/m²

total wall area	**W**	
total glazing area	**G**	
total floor area	**F**	
south glazing area	**S**	
separating wall area	**B**	
ratio	**G/W**	
ratio	**S/F**	
ratio	**B/F**	

information

RESULTS F

base case	
option 1	
option 2	
option 3	

50 100 150   annual energy Kwh/m²

INFILTRATION B

0 1 2
air–changes per hour

B1

SOLAR + CASUAL GAINS C

no casual gains

0%   4%   8%12%
16%

S/F

0 50 100   Kwh/m²

BUFFER SPACE D

100
50

BOILER EFFICIENCY E

100%
80%
60%
40%

LT4 WORKSHEET March 95

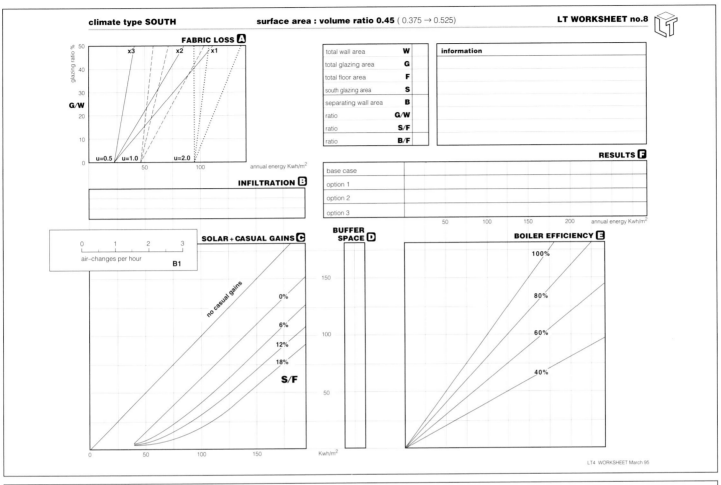

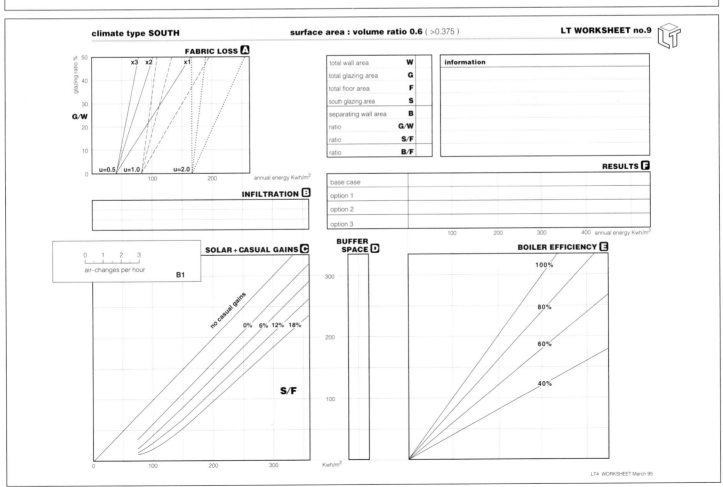

11   WORKED EXAMPLE

An eight-storey slab block located in Berlin is constructed of concrete panels with styrafoam-filled cavity. The units are double aspect, the main facades facing N and S. About 35% of both main facades are glazed with double glazing. Every unit has a 6m wide balcony on the south facade. The building is 12m deep, 24m high and 40m wide. It is heated from a shared boiler which serves the group of 7 blocks. The heating plant has recently been refurbished.

The general condition of the windows and fabric is poor and the building is very draughty. (Indoor temperatures drop noticeably in cold windy weather indicating a very high infiltration rate.) It is on an exposed site (relative to the building height) Due to quality control problems during manufacture, degradation of the styrafoam and cold bridging effects, the panels are known to have a U-value of about 1.5. The same is assumed for the roof.

11.1 BASE CASE

Select the LT Worksheet for (surface area) / (volume) ratio 0.3 and climate zone NE Continental.

Total surface area	= 3456
Total volume	= 11520
Ratio surface area/volume	0.3
Climate zone	NE
Total wall area W	= 2496
Total glazing area G	
G = .35 x 24 x 40 x 2 = 672	
Total floor area (gross) F	= 3840
South glazing area S	= 336

Enter this data into the panel on the worksheet.

Enter chart **A** with the ratio of total glazing area to total wall area G/A, about 27%, and rule a horizontal line in feint pencil. By interpolating, find the point halfway between the double glazed (x2) line for U-value 1.0 and U-value 2.0, then drop a vertical line down to chart **B**. Where it crosses the axis gives the annual useful heating energy for fabric losses only.

Estimate infiltration from Table 1. For *exposed* we get a factor of 1.3 which we multiply the sum of 10 for pre-cast slab construction with dry lining and 8 for poorly fitting windows (but lobby access). This give 2.3 ac/h. Measure this off from the scale (make a mark on the edge of a piece of paper) and transfer this to the top line of chart **B**, along a line to the right. From the end drop a vertical line down to chart **C**. The new value on the horizontal axis will be the gross annual useful heating energy per square metre, without the benefit of internal gains and solar gains. Note what a large contribution overventilation makes to heat loss from this kind of building.

All buildings benefit from internal gains (from people, lighting, cooking and losses from domestic hot water etc.) during the heating season. To estimate the effect of these from the intercept with the 0% line draw a line horizontally on to charts **D** and **E**. But most buildings also can benefit from solar energy, depending upon (a) what fraction of glazing faces south (or within 45° of south) and (b) if the heating controls respond to the presence of solar gain by reducing the auxiliary heating input. The ratio of south-facing glazing area to total floor area is about 9% for this building, so chose this curve and from the intercept draw a horizontal line on to the next chart. Note however, this is the maximum solar contribution. To achieve this the heat emitters in each room would require thermostatic valves.

Since we do not have a sunspace in the base case we move on to chart **E**. So far, the energy has been calculated as useful heat, i.e. that which is actually used in the room. If we want to know the heating fuel amounts or costs, we have to allow for combustion losses by the boiler and in losses in delivering the heat to the building. Chart **E** plots the ratio of delivered energy to useful energy for a range of system efficiencies. Referring to Table 3 we estimate the efficiency to be about 60%.

Where the horizontal line intersects the 60% line, draw a vertical line upwards to the top line of the Results chart **F**. This now gives delivered energy for the base case. We can add onto this bar the extra energy needed if solar energy were not used (working back from the 0% solar line) indicating the range of influence of the control system.

11.2 REFURBISHMENT OPTIONS

Three options have been drawn on the chart. The first reduced the fabric losses from a U value of 1.5 to a U value of 0.5 by overcladding. The reduced fabric loss is then carried through the charts as before. In the next option the infiltration is reduced by weatherstripping from 2.3 to 1.5.

The final option to be assessed is a sunspace. We will propose that the 6m wide south-facing balcony be glazed-in.

The starting point is to calculate the separating wall area, that is the *total* area between the sunspaces formed by the glazed-in balcony, and the heated part of the building. From the elevation we determine that 60% of the south facade will be protected. (Note that it is not the actual area of glass, but if this is less than half of the separating wall, then an average of the glass area and the separating wall area should be taken.) Since we are dealing with energy per metre squared of floor area, we have to express this as a ratio.

Separating wall area B = 40 x 24 x .6 = 576
B/F = .15

Next, refer to Table 2 selecting the North East climate zone and the Balcony type buffer space. Assuming that the separating wall insulation is between medium and good, the thermal saving for the buffer (SB) is 81 kWh/m^2 (i.e. interpolating between 102 and 60). If the sunspace is designed for solar ventilation preheating (SVP) then the savings are 157 kWh/m^2 (i.e. between 178 and 136). Let us be optimistic and assume the latter. Multiply this value by B/F to arrive at the thermal savings: 157 x 0.15 = 23.6 kWh/m^2.

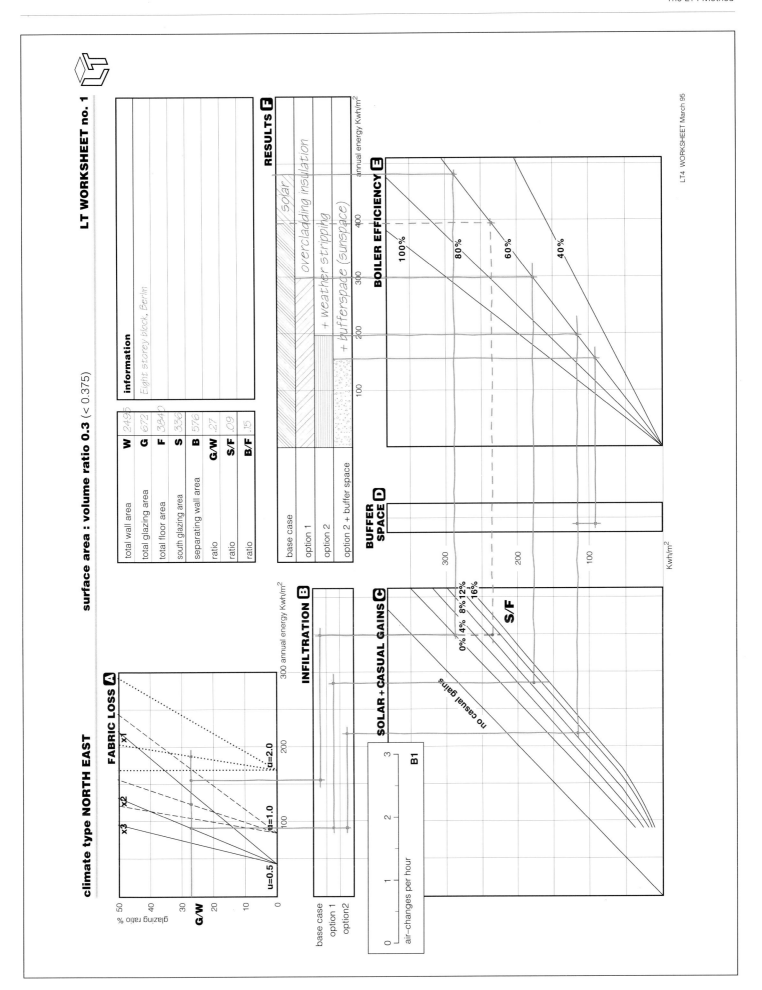

This represents the annual saving of the sunspace per square metre of floor area, and is thus compatible with the chart. Subtract this amount on chart D. The actual amount may look disappointingly small but it is about 20% of the total remaining heating demand. Also, the sunspace is not just of energy saving value, but will increase the usefulness of that space.

If the sunspace is heated by the occupants, by leaving the door open, provided the sunspace glazing and wall specification is as good as the main wall, the energy use will be no worse than before. Since this use cannot be prevented, it might be a good strategy to insulate the balcony wall and use at least double glazing.

The final result is quite dramatic, reducing the annual energy from about 400 kWh/m² to about 150kWh/m².

12   LT OVERHEATING PREDICTOR FOR MULTI-RESIDENTIAL BUILDINGS

This procedure gives an indication of the probability that overheating will cause dissatisfaction to the occupants. It can be seen as a kind of checklist where the items have been giving a weighting to reflect their relative importance.

It is organised as *effective gains* and *effective losses*. Gains are mainly from solar radiation through windows. Losses are due to ventilation and the combination of ventilation and mass and are represented by negative values. A final score is calculated by a simple arithmetic procedure and compared with a target value appropriate for the climate zone.

Procedure

With reference to the letters appearing on the chart:

G1   Select the appropriate description of the glazing for the main glazed facade. Large means greater than 50% of facade is glazed, small is less than 20%. If there are more than one facade with significant area, describe the west- facing in preference to south or east-facing, and south or east-facing, in preference to north-facing. Transfer the score to the right-hand column.

f1   Select the orientation and transfer the factor to the right-hand column. Note that west-facing glazing has most effect because of the low sun angle and the fact that the gains occur when the air temperature is the highest.

f2   Select the shading type. These factors are in effect transmission factors. They are default values; use different values if they can be obtained for the *actual* shading devices.

Note that **G1** should be multiplied by **f1** and **f2**.

G2 & G3   Solar gains may occur through uninsulated fabric,

particularly into spaces beneath an uninsulated roof. Reduced values could be used for highly reflective or well insulated external finishes.

G4   This is a compulsory score representing gains from occupants and equipment.

L1   Select cross-ventilation or single-sided ventilation. If the building is in the central or southern zone use the lower values; ventilation is less effective at the time of peak overheating risk because the outside temperature is often well above the comfort temperature.

L2   Wind-driven ventilation will obviously be compromised in sheltered sites, so this value is positive.

L3   The presence of a ceiling or desk fan has a local cooling effect and is thus equivalent to a heat loss.

L4   Thermal mass, particularly if cooled at night, is an important method of removing heat at the time of day when there is most risk of overheating.

The score is calculated as follows:

score = G1 x f1 x f2 + G2 + G3 + G4 + L1 + L2 + L3 + L4

Note that there should be only one value for each lettered box. Also note that the method does not distinguish between, for example, adequate and inadequate cross-ventilation. The assumption is made that it is adequate. What this means in design terms will be found in the Design Guidelines.

For the purpose of this assessment, the three temperature zones, North-east, Central and Southern, are defined by the average temperature of the hottest month being (1) less than 18°C (2) from 18°C to 22°C, and (3) greater than 22°C, respectively. If the final score is greater than the criterion for the zone, as shown below, then overheating is likely to cause dissatisfaction when considered over the summer period. Note that satisfying the criterion does not imply that overheating will *never* take place.

North-east	3.0
Central	1.5
Southern	0.5

	WINDOWS			
G1	large		6	
	or medium		4	
	or small		2	
	ORIENTATION			
f1	West		1	
	or South or East		0.5	
	or North		0.2	
	SHADING			
f2	movable external		0.2	
	or movable internal		0.5	
	or fixed		0.7	
	or none		1	

G2	fabric gains (wall)	1	
G3	fabric gains (roof)	1.5	
G4	internal gains	2	2

	VENTILATION + MASS	North East	South Central	
L1	cross – ventilation	-2	-1	
	or single – sided ventilation	-1	0	
L2	very sheltered site		+1	
L3	ceiling fan		-1	
L4	light – weight		0	
	or heavy – weight		-2	
	or heavy – weight and night ventilation		-3	
	TOTAL			

CRITERIA		
NORTHERN		3.0
CENTRAL		1.5
SOUTH		0.5

LT Overheating Predictor for multi-residential buildings

B E R L I N
GERMANY

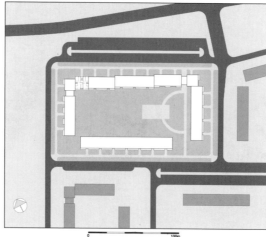

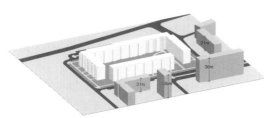

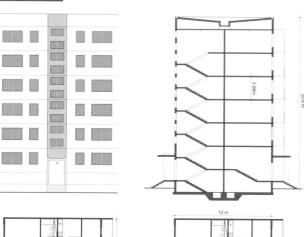

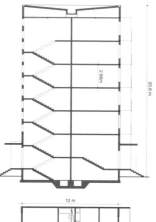

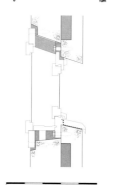

Site Location and Description

The site is located to the north east of Berlin in the residential area of Marzhan. To the North is the busy Wuhletalstrasse, to the east an open grassed area, to the west an industrial zone, and apartment buildings of varying heights to the south. The chosen apartment buildings are six storeys above basement located on four sides of an open space. Berlin is located within the LT4 Climatic Zone area 'NORTH EAST'. The buildings have a 'high' exposure.

Construction

Apartments run the full depth of the building (12.0m) and are 6.0m wide, seperated by 2.4m wide stairways. The external walls are constructed of 260mm thick-triple layer prefabricated panels, comprising a 60mm thick external reinforced concrete panel, 50mm polystyrene insulation and a 150mm thick internal reinforced concrete panel and is dry lined. The U value is 1.5 W/m²K. The internal load bearing walls are constructed of 150mm thick prefabricated reinforced concrete panels, and non load bearing walls are 60mm thick reinforced concrete panels. The floors are 140mm thick pre-stressed concrete panels with a 25mm screed. The roof is constructed of two reinforced concrete panels, with an

inaccessible void of 1450mm measured at the eaves. The inner panel is constructed of 140mm thick pre-stressed concrete with 50mm insulation above. The outer concrete panel, with waterproof covering, drains to a central gutter. Windows are constructed of plastic-coated timber and are double glazed.

Services

A district heating system supplies low pressure hot water (LPHW) radiators and domestic hot water (DHW) via a sub-station in each apartment block, and is well maintained.

Problems

- Deterioration of panels, cracking and flaking of concrete.
- Thermal bridging at panel joints.
- Damage to floor screeds through use.
- Insufficent insulation generally and lack of noise insulation.
- Absence of lifts causes hardship.

This Competition is arranged within the **INNOBUILD** Project of the **European Commission Directorate-General XII** for Science Research and Development.

BOURGAS
BULGARIA

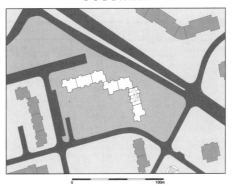

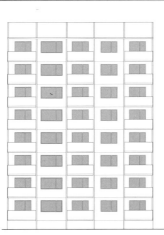

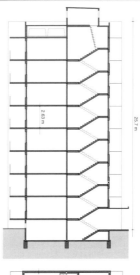

Site Location and Description

The site is located on the busy route from the city of Sofia to its industrial zone. This route continues to the Black Sea. The housing estate 'Bratya Miladinovi', where the apartment block is located, was constructed in the last twenty years. The chosen apartment buildings form a group of seven blocks comprising six eight-storey blocks and one seven-storey block to the west. Two of the eight-storey blocks have open circulation routes through the buildings at ground floor level. Bourgas is located within the LT4 Climatic Zone area 'SOUTH'. The buildings have a 'medium' exposure.

Construction

The complex is typical of Bulgarian mass residential building of the 1970s and 1980s, with prefabricated walls, floors and roofs manufactured locally and assembled on site. Longitudinal bays are 3.6m wide and overall building width is 9.96m. The external walls are constructed of 240mm thick triple-layer prefabricated concrete panels, comprising 90mm thick external reinforced concrete panel rendered externally, 60mm thick polystyrene insulation and a 70mm thick internal reinforced concrete panel with 1-3mm plaster. The U value is 1.2W/m²K. The internal load bearing walls are constructed of 140mm thick prefabricated concrete panels. Internal non-load bearing walls are 60mm thick. The floors are constructed of 140mm thick prefabricated concrete slabs with 22mm screed. The roof is constructed of two concrete panels with a 1.3m inaccessible void between. The inner reinforced concrete panel is 140mm thick with 50mm polystyrene insulation above the slab and covered with 25mm mortar. The outer

reinforced concrete panel is 100mm thick with a weatherproof covering. Floor and ceiling insulation is only applied below first floor and above top floor apartments. Rainwater is drained at the perimeter. Double glazed windows are constructed of timber frames cast into the reinforced concrete wall panels.

Services

A lift is provided in each block. A central heating plant was envisaged for the basement, but never installed. Individual stoves and electric heaters are provided in the apartments. Hot water is provided by electric boilers in each apartment.

Problems

- Inaccuracy of panel joints causes rain penetration.
- Deterioration of door and window frames.
- Polystyrene insulation, of inadequate thickness, has often been broken when installed, and has shrunk with time, resulting in cold bridging.
- Balcony roofs are poorly insulated, causing condensation.

This Competition is arranged within the **INNOBUILD** Project of the **European Commission Directorate-General XII** for Science Research and Development.

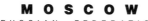

MOSCOW
RUSSIAN FEDERATION

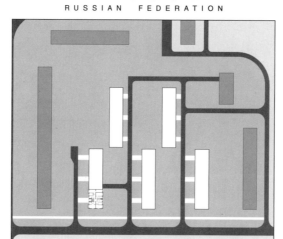

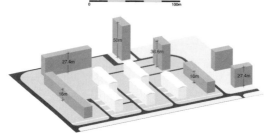

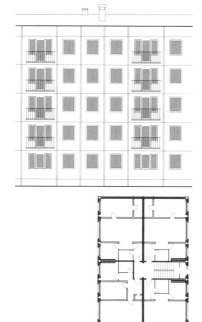

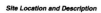

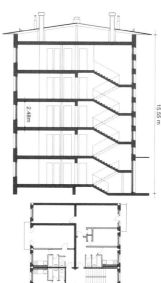

Site Location and Description

The site is located to the north-west of Moscow in the residential district of 'Golovinsky'. The Moscow-Leningrad highway lies to the west, with the 'Park of Friendship' situated to the north. This area was developed during 1960 to 1980 with some industrial buildings, and mixed-height apartments of nine to sixteen stories to the north, and five storey to the east and west. Poolkovskaya road, directly to the south, carries light traffic. The chosen apartment buildings are five storeys high. Moscow is located within the LT4 Climatic Zone area 'NORTH EAST'. The buildings have a 'medium' exposure.

Construction

These 'first generation' system buildings are constructed of prefabricated reinforced concrete walls, floors, and roofs. Longitudinal bays are 6.0m width with 2.4m stair bays and overall building width is 11.6m. The external walls are constructed of 400mm thick aerated reinforced concrete panels without insulation, but plastered internally. The U value is 2.0 W/m²K. The internal load bearing walls are constructed of 250mm thick aerated reinforced concrete panels. The floors are constructed of 220mm thick multi-cavity aerated reinforced concrete panels, with a 30mm

screed. The roof is a pitched rafter roof constructed in timber and tiled. The roof void has a minimum height of 700mm above the subroof, which consist of 220mm thick multi-cavity aerated reinforced concrete panels with 140mm of fibre glass insulating boards placed above the roof panels and covered with a 30mm thick screed. Windows and doors are timber framed, and are double glazed.

Services

A district heating system supplies low pressure (LPHW) radiators and domestic hot water (DHW) via a central boiler in each building and is well maintained.

Problems

- Poor sealing of panel joints allows rain penetration.
- Poor spatial arrangement and sizing of rooms.
- Small bathrooms and corridors.
- Lack of thermal and sound insulation.
- Absence of lifts causes hardship.

This Competition is arranged within the **INNOBUILD** Project of the **European Commission Directorate-General XII** for Science Research and Development.

P É C S
H U N G A R Y

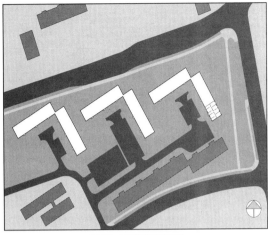

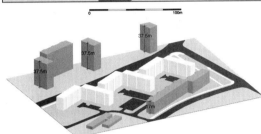

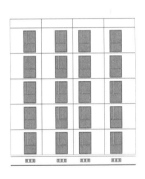

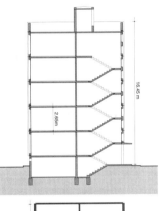

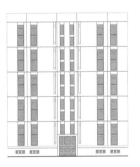

Site Location and Description

The site is situated to the west of the city of Pécs in a residential area consisting of single family housing and apartment buildings varying from five to eleven storeys with an adjacent supermarket, creche, kindergarten and school. The chosen apartment buildings, constructed in the 1960s, are five and six stories high over basements, surrounded by roads on three sides and similar apartment buildings to the west.

Pécs is located within the LT4 Climatic Zone area 'CENTRAL'. The buildings have a 'high' exposure.

Construction

The building is constructed of loadbearing prefabricated concrete panels, with longitudinal bays 3.6m, and an overall building width of 10.65m. The external wall is constructed of 250mm thick triple-layer prefabricated panels, composed of a light ceramic composite concrete between two dense RC layers, with a thin plaster layer internally. The U value is 1.7 W/m²K. The internal load-bearing walls are 150mm thick. Internal non-loadbearing walls are 60mm thick. The floors are constructed of 120mm thick reinforced concrete panels with 30mm mineral wool insulation and 45mm thick screed. Roofs are constructed of 120mm thick reinforced concrete panels,

with 340mm to 130mm thick screed laid to a fall, covered by ceramic slabs and bituminous felt. Rainwater is drained to the centre of the roof. Double timber-framed windows are fitted, each frame is single-glazed.

Services

A District heating system supplies low pressure hot water (LPHW) radiators and domestic hot water (DHW) via a substation in each apartment block, and is poorly maintained.

Problems

- Poor sealing of panel joints allows rain penetration, and there is also water penetration through panel surfaces.
- Roof leaks are caused by the detioration of the roofing felt with age.
- Apartments are very small, with no balconies, dining areas and inadequate storage.
- Absence of lifts cause hardship.

This Competition is arranged within the **INNOBUILD** Project of the **European Commission Directorate-General XII** for Science Research and Development.

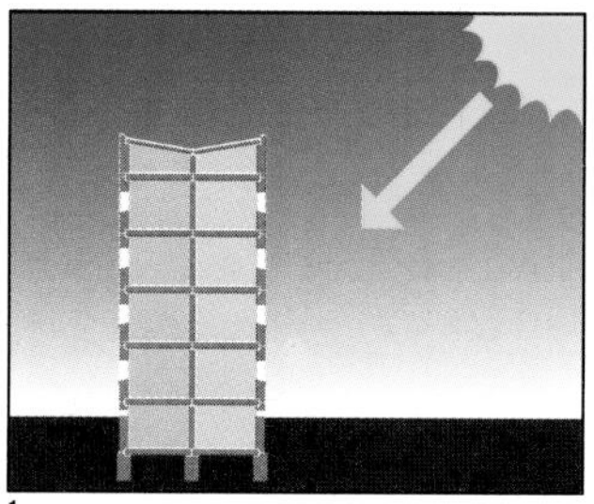
1

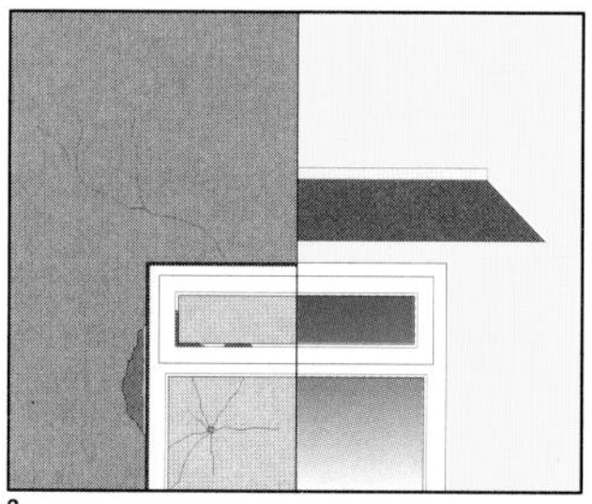
2

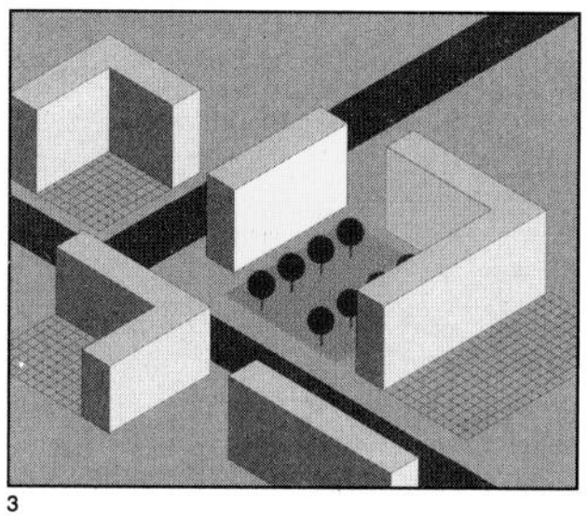
3

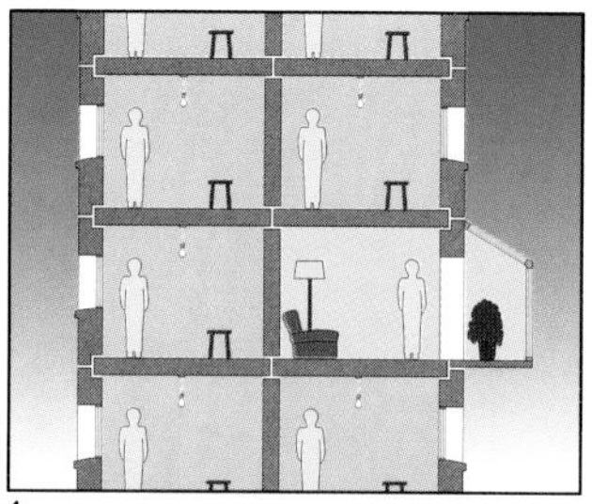
4

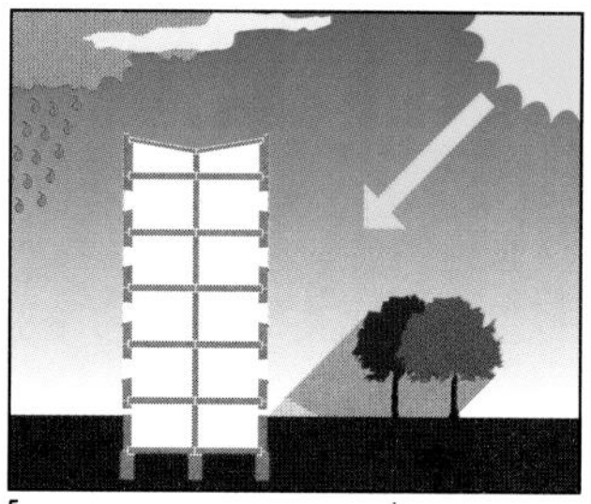
5

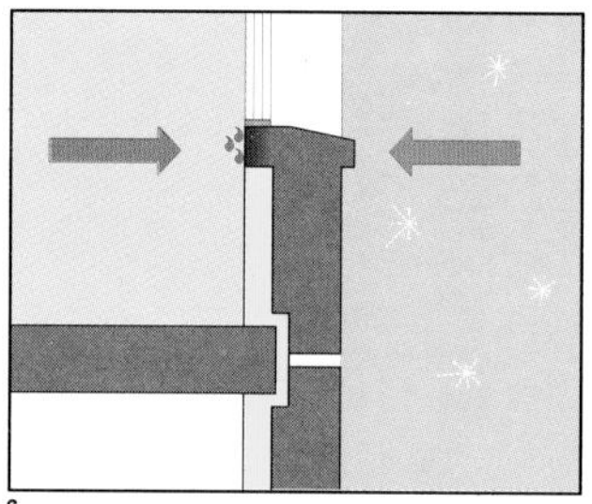
6

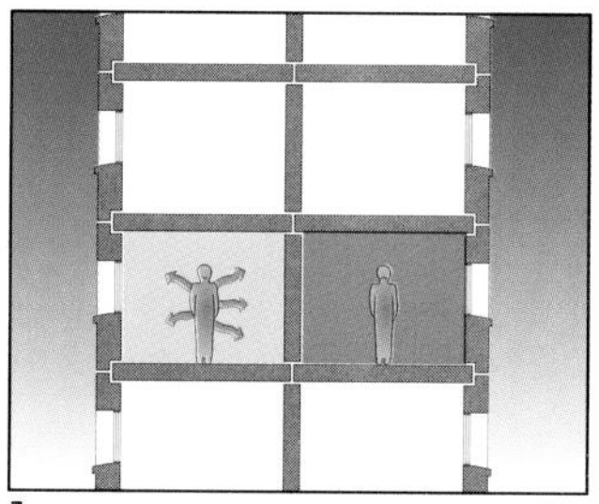
7

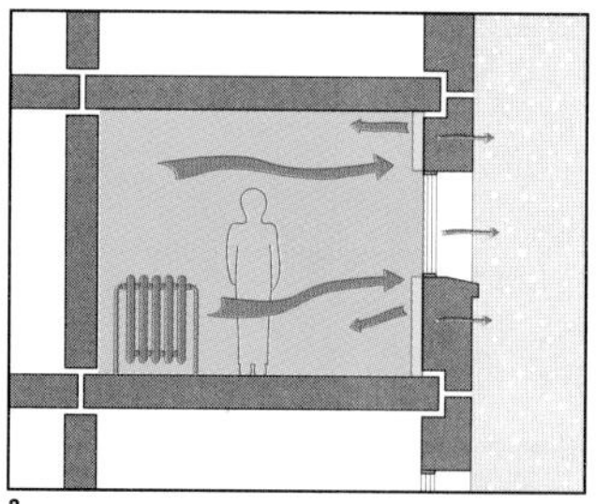
8

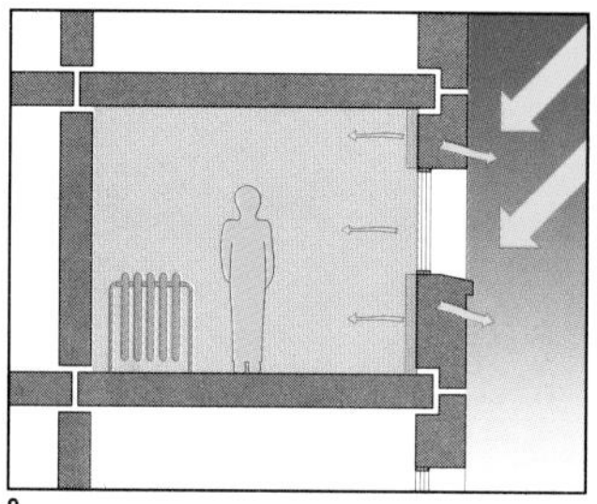
9

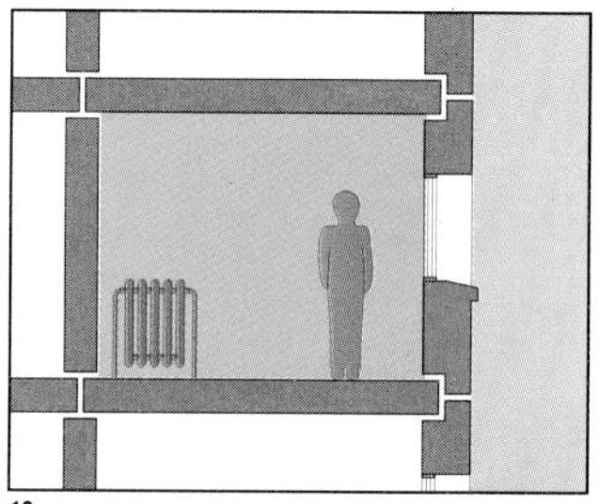
10

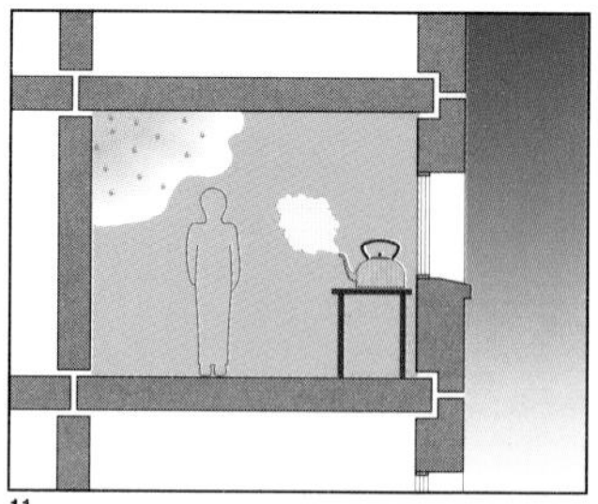
11

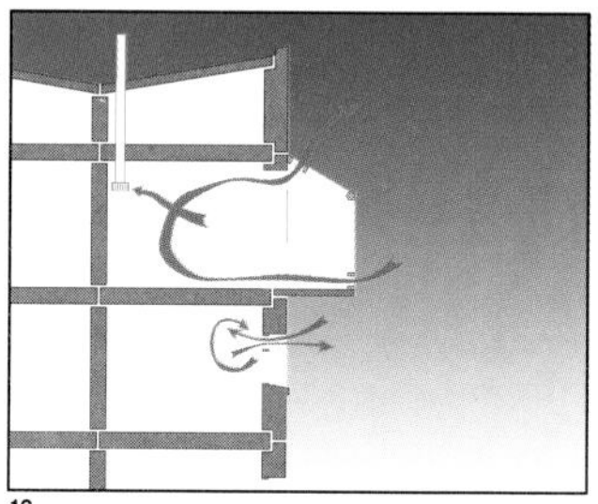
12

DESIGN GUIDELINES

These guidelines aim to provide an overview of design issues relevant to the energy-efficient remodelling of post-War multi-storey apartment buildings in Europe. They present a strategy which architects may follow to examine energy, constructional, and indoor environmental problems; and a range of energy-efficient, environmentally benign design measures which can improve heating, cooling and lighting in apartment buildings. [1]

DESIGN STRATEGY

If a building is to be upgraded due to physical deterioration, the potential for architectural improvements is considerable and may extend to the redefinition of the functional and spatial arrangement of the building or combination of adjacent buildings, including the design of the individual apartments and adjacent spaces; we are not limited simply to a re-design of the facades. The benefits to occupants from a thorough re-evaluation of the building's design and operation are potentially far-reaching, and affect not only indoor comfort conditions but also health, prestige, aesthetic satisfaction, amenity, capital value, security from energy price fluctuations and effects on the global and local environment. Therefore. it may not be adequate to estimate pay-back simply in terms of money saved on energy and running costs related to investment cost. [2]

Design changes at the neighbourhood scale, involving several buildings and their adjacent spaces, can offer interesting architectural, functional and energy-saving possibilities while enhancing urban quality. The spaces between buildings may be exploited to good effect, for example, through landscaping to optimise microclimatic conditions for energy saving and comfort; or by structures which link buildings and provide additional enclosed areas. [3]

When a building is being improved, it is reasonable to combine measures to save energy with improvements in architectural quality, comfort levels, and with measures to increase the lifespan of the building. Where possible, desired thermal and visual comfort levels should be provided by passive means: by improvements in the thermal and visual performance of the building itself, rather than by mechanical means. Where mechanical heating or ventilation are to be provided, the energy required should be supplied from renewable sources rather than from fossil fuels. The use of mechanical air conditioners, which can result in the consumption of large quantities of primary energy, should be avoided by minimising unwanted heat gains and by the use of natural forms of cooling where possible. [4]

As a first step, consider the nature and extent of adverse or beneficial micro-climatic conditions occurring around the building. Patterns of solar radiation, temperature, precipitation. wind flow and strength, topography, vegetation, adjacent buildings and the nature of local activities should be studied and interpreted in terms of desired environmental conditions both indoors and outdoors, and opportunities to enhance the positive features. [5]

While the lighting performance of residential buildings, including the use of daylight, may not have as significant an effect on the amount of energy used as would be the case in office buildings, the quality of light is an important consideration for the comfort and well-being of occupants and the way in which the architecture of the spaces is modelled.

An analysis of the energy performance of the existing building in a 'free running' state should be carried out for representative periods of the day and year, together with an investigation of the causes of any building failures (such as cold bridging or condensation) to understand how the building performs and to provide a reference or 'base case' from which to design. The thermal performance of the existing building envelope should be analysed in terms of unwanted heat losses (or gains) through walls, windows, doors, floors (especially the ground floor), and the roof. Particular attention might be paid to the effectiveness of existing insulation; to cold bridges, especially at balconies and floor-to-external wall joints where insulation may be deficient; and to energy losses due to the unwanted infiltration of cold external air (or heat gains due to warm air in summer). The LT Method offers a means of analysing the performance of the existing building (the base case), and comparing the effects of design proposals on energy use. [6]

When considering what architectural interventions may be made, it is appropriate to test their effects on the thermal and lighting performance of the building. For example, systems which protect the building from the effects of weather can have significant architectural implications.

When remodelling has been completed, it is essential that close supervision and briefing of the construction team takes place and that building occupants are provided with concise, easily-understood explanations of how the thermal and lighting systems can be operated most effectively, what is required of them in using the building, and the likely results of failure to operate or maintain the building and its energy systems appropriately.

THERMAL COMFORT

The improvement of indoor thermal comfort and health conditions may take precedence over economic concerns for the improvement of the energy performance of a building. Indeed, where thermal comfort conditions are deficient, it is likely that some of the potential energy savings which can result from building renovation will be absorbed by improvements in indoor comfort levels, and this must be accounted for in any cost-benefit analysis. Maintaining a notionally acceptable mean indoor air temperature may not suffice as draughts, cold surfaces and humidity levels may prevent adequate levels of comfort being reached. [7,8,9]

INDOOR TEMPERATURE

An object will radiate heat to another object at a lower temperature. This exchange of energy may occur, for example, between a person and a nearby cold surface such as a window. In poorly insulated buildings this phenomenon requires unnecessarily high indoor air temperatures to compensate these radiant losses. Insulation of the building envelope can reduce the temperature required to satisfy comfort requirements. [10]

Excessive variations in room air temperatures, for example between ankle and head level, can result in discomfort. Cold surfaces, such as windows or uninsulated walls, can absorb radiated heat from people and can cause convective draughts, both of which lead to discomfort.

RELATIVE HUMIDITY

As the level of relative humidity in the air increases, its capacity to absorb excess heat and moisture is reduced. Relative humidity (RH) in the range 30 to 70% may be quite acceptable for human comfort, but to avoid condensation in winter RH should remain between 35 and 55%. Increased ventilation may be needed where the RH is excessively high. Indoor factors which increase RH include cooking, washing and moisture produced by occupants. [11]

VENTILATION FOR COMFORT

While minimum air change rates of 0.5 to 1.0 per hour (ACH) may be required to provide adequate fresh air in occupied rooms, excessive and uncontrolled air movement (often caused by air infiltration through poorly sealed window and door frames) can seriously reduce perceived thermal comfort, especially in cold weather, and result in a need for higher indoor temperatures. In summer, increased ventilation rates may be required (see Cooling section) which supply more than adequate fresh air without diminishing comfort indoors. An increase of 1 K in air temperature can result in 10% extra energy use. With excessively low air change rates (typically below 0.5 ACH) condensation, mould growth and other health problems may result. Considerably higher air change rates may be required in densely occupied living rooms, or occasionally in bathrooms and kitchens.

The heat loss (in Watts) due to ventilation may be calculated using the formula:

$1/3 NV\Delta T = W$ where
N= number of air changes per hour
V= volume of the heated space (m^3)
ΔT= internal - external temperature difference (K)

Room	Temp °C	Temp. diff. walls/room floor/room	Relative humidity	Air velocity m/s
Living room	21		Summer:	
Bedroom	18		30 - 70%	Winter: <0.15
Bathroom	22	<3		
Toilets	18	(Winter)	Winter:	Summer:0.25
Staircases / halls		16		<50%

Recommended temperatures, RHs air velocities in different rooms in residential buildings. Source: ISO 7730 (1984)

Although single-sided ventilation, usually through windows in the same wall, may introduce a significant volume of fresh air into the room, it will not achieve as effective a replacement of all of the air in the room as cross ventilation assisted by appropriately placed openings such as windows, stacks and vents. Natural ventilation is driven by the action of wind and temperature differences between indoors and outdoors, and is affected by factors such as the height of air outlets above inlets, internal resistance to airflow, location and flow resistance characteristics of openings in the building envelope, local terrain, and the immediate shelter surrounding the building. [12]

Openable windows offer limited control of ventilation, usually allowing room air to be purged instead of supplying a constant level of fresh air. Special openings (such as finely adjustable trickle vents) can, in conjunction with windows, help to ensure a controlled level of ventilation and minimise condensation without incurring a significant energy penalty.

Passive stack ventilation systems provide more control over natural ventilation, as vertical stacks (air ducts) terminating in the negative pressure region above the roof may be used to extract room pollutants and moisture. Replacement air is supplied through purpose-designed openings (trickle vents) in the building envelope. Stacks can be located away from inlets to encourage cross ventilation, and should be as near vertical as possible. Neither need they be intrusive, with typical diameters of around 100mm to 150mm per dwelling.

Advanced natural ventilation systems offer the possibilities of recovering heat from expelled air, pre-heating (or cobling) replacement air, and adjusting air supply in response to indoor temperature, humidity or CO_2 levels.

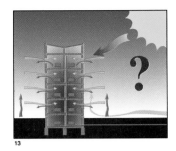

13

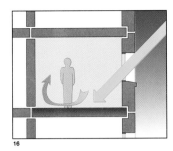

16

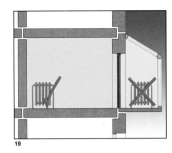

19

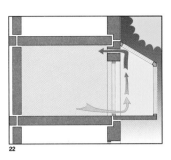

22

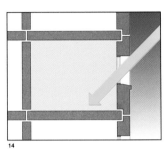

14

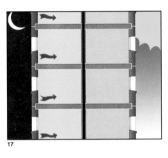

17

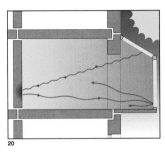

20

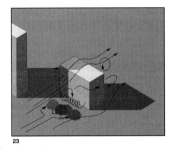

23

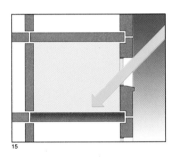

15

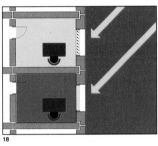

18

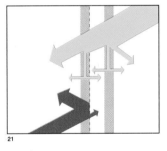

21

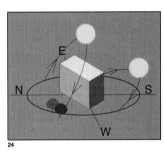

24

HEATING STRATEGY

The following measures can help to reduce energy used by conventional heating systems:

- **Solar Collection:** solar energy is collected and converted into heat.
- **Heat Storage:** Heat is collected during sunny periods and stored for future use.
- **Heat Distribution:** collected heat is distributed to the parts of the building which require heating.
- **Heat Conservation:** heat is retained in the building for as long as possible.

Exploitation of these principles can, in appropriate circumstances, make use of an auxiliary heating system unnecessary for much of the year. The auxiliary system should be appropriately sized to take account of solar heat and to operate efficiently when supplementary heating is required. [13,14,15,16,17]

SOLAR COLLECTION

Transparent elements

Solar gains through vertical glazing vary with orientation and glazing characteristics. South-facing surfaces receive more solar radiation in winter and less in summer when compared with surfaces at other orientations. This is approximately in phase with the heating requirements. Throughout the year, the solar gains through west and south-west glazing are very similar to those through glazing facing east and south-east. In summer, windows facing west can give rise to overheating if they are not protected from the sun's rays, which are at a low angle of incidence, since they receive radiation at the hottest time of the day. [18]

Glazing tilted at a low angle to the horizontal (e.g. 30 degrees) can cause overheating in summer despite the fact that it gives low gains in winter. In general, such glazing should be avoided unless it can be shaded when necessary. It can, however, be used in sunspaces or atria if they are partitioned from the other occupied spaces in the building and have their own ventilation systems.

Any auxiliary heating of a sun space will destroy the benefits of solar heating and will change the sun space from an energy saving feature into an energy wasting one. It is necessary to separate the sunspace from the rest of the building. Doors in the separating wall should remain closed whenever possible. [19]

Opaque elements

The concept of collecting heat through walls is mainly applicable to warmer regions where there is a need for heating only at night but thermal insulation is not necessary. In Northern Europe, more heat will be lost through an uninsulated south-facing wall than can ever be collected from the sun. In colder parts of Europe where outside walls must be insulated, the insulation prevents the diffusion of heat into the wall.

Greenhouse effect

The greenhouse effect results from a process whereby short-wave solar energy is collected through glazing, absorbed by opaque elements in the building, and re-emitted as long wave radiation which is prevented by the glazing from leaving the building. [20]

The efficiency of this collecting system is affected by its geometry, the characteristics of the glazing (for example, the percentage of glazed area and the material's spectral transmission curve) and properties of the solid elements which receive solar radiation, such as solar absorptance and spectral thermal emission. [21]

With double glazing, the total transmission is lower than with single glazing. The emission from the walls behind the glazing will therefore be reduced, since less radiation strikes them but more heat will be retained. With low-emissivity glass, (a selective coating reduces the transmission of long wave radiation to the outside), transmission will be lower still but a greater proportion of the thermal energy will be retained in the building.

HEAT STORAGE

Direct storage

When solar radiation strikes a material - either directly or after transmission through glass - part of it is absorbed, transformed into heat and stored in the mass of the material. The material heats up progressively by conduction as the heat diffuses through.

Heat penetration is quickest in materials with a high thermal diffusion coefficient. This increases with increasing conductivity. Thermal diffusion in the material prevents the surface temperature from rising rapidly when radiation falls on it and causes the temperature of the entire mass to increase. Materials with high heat storage capacity such as concrete, brick and water heat up and cool down relatively slowly. Thermal insulating materials such as glass fibre and foam, usually because of their open or cellular structure, form poor heat stores and diffuse heat very badly.

Indirect storage

Indirect storage occurs when a building component is heated up by absorption of heat radiated from other, warmer components (such as walls and floors) or by convection from the surrounding air. Indirect storage is influenced by the temperature difference between the components, their location and emissivities. Unlike visible radiation, the emission of infra-red radiation is not affected by the colour of the surface. It is, however, influenced by surface condition, and whether metallic or non-metallic. Indirect storage through convection is influenced by the temperature difference between the air and the component, by the speed of the air and the roughness of the component surface. Rough surfaces have a greater area and therefore assist convective heat transfer.

Use can be made of a remote storage system to accumulate heat transferred from a sunspace for instance by fans and air ducts, and to diffuse heat to the building in a controlled way, as required. This will only be effective if the store is adequately sized and well insulated so that a significant increase in store temperature is achieved. Fans will consume some power. It is better to locate a mass store within a building so that any heat loss can be collected by the building.

The heat stored in a unit volume of material per degree of temperature rise is its specific heat capacity. Dense materials (stone, concrete, brick etc.) are typically chosen for heat storage. Materials with good thermal conductivity accumulate and lose heat quickly. In a lightweight building or where increased storage is required without the use of massive materials, high heat storage capacity materials can be used. Examples are water (1.157 kWh/m³ at 20⁰ C), and phase-change materials which make use of the latent heat of fusion, that is the heat required to change the state of the material from a solid to a liquid without a change in temperature. Very large quantities of heat (typically 38 to 105 kWh/m³) can be stored when the phase change occurs, therefore much smaller volumes are required.

HEAT DISTRIBUTION

Ideally a passive solar building should provide heat directly to the areas where it will be used, thus requiring no distribution system. However, this is not always possible as in the case of north facing rooms, but can be achieved by natural or mechanical means.

In natural distribution, stored heat is transmitted by convection and radiation. Convection occurs when the surface temperature of the storage material is above ambient. Long wave infra red radiation emission takes place when the surface temperature of the storage material is higher than the surface temperature of neighbouring objects. The diffusion of heat will be almost immediate on the side exposed to the radiation. On the opposite side, however, there will be a time delay before heat is released. The delay is influenced by the thermal inertia of the wall, and its extent depends on the dimensions and physical properties of the wall.

When the inside face of the wall reaches an appropriate temperature, the air of the space beyond will be heated by convection and surfaces near the wall will be heated by radiation. This delayed heat transfer process can help to maintain comfortable temperatures for a significant length of time after the solar radiation has ceased.

Thermo-circulation

When air is heated, its density decreases and it tends to rise. This phenomenon can be used to distribute heat generated by solar gain in one zone to another, cooler zone. Meanwhile, cooler air in contact with the irradiated surface is heated. An air circulation loop is thus set up between the zone which is directly heated by solar radiation and the non-irradiated zones, if the organisation of spaces permits this. [22]

MICRO-CLIMATE

The micro-climatic conditions around a building are influenced by the general, macro-climatic characteristics of the region, modified at the site by topographical features, vegetation, shelter, shading and the effects of adjacent buildings and some activities. There may be considerable scope to take advantage of favourable micro-climatic effects and to minimise unfavourable ones.

Once the characteristics of the macro-climate are known in terms of daily and seasonal variations in air and ground temperature, solar radiation, humidity, precipitation, wind strength and direction, and cloud cover, an investigation of micro-climatic conditions at the site may be undertaken to characterise the influences of local features such as topography, vegetation, adjacent buildings etc. Existing patterns of solar radiation and shading, wind flows and strengths, shelter and precipitation may be analysed and optimised to improve indoor comfort and energy use. Examples of interventions include: changes to ground contours (earth berming, etc.); planting of trees and other vegetation for shelter or shading; and changes in the reflective characteristics of external surfaces, including the ground, which can improve daylight levels indoors. [23,24]

25

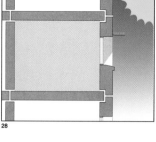

28

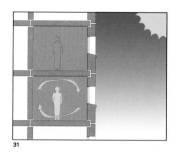

31

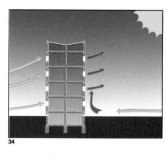

34

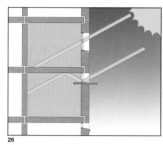

26

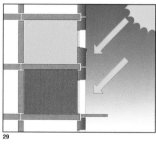

29

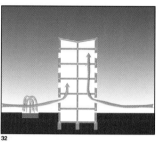

32

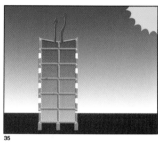

35

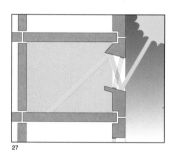

27

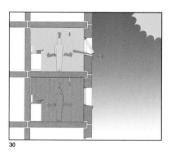

30

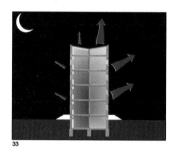

33

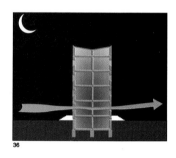

36

LIGHTING STRATEGY

Daylighting design involves the provision of natural daylight in the interiors of buildings to reduce or eliminate daytime use of electric lights, thereby offering sometimes substantial savings in energy use and consequent environmental damage; and if skilfully executed, can provide healthier and more pleasant living conditions.

Research shows that people like the variety of daylight, enjoy the presence of sunlight in a building, and want at least a glimpse of the world outside. Daylight is the light to which we are naturally adapted; it is the light against which we measure all other kinds of light, in which we try to view things if we want to know what they really 'look' like. Historically. fine buildings have always exploited natural light. After a brief interlude, the skilful use of daylight is again being seen as a critical element in the design of buildings of high architectural quality.

Good electric lighting design and control can reduce energy use significantly, but a more fundamental and rewarding approach to the problem is to first design or modify the form of the building to allow it to admit and evenly distribute sufficient natural light to all of the occupied space. Often, in conventional buildings, there will already be more than adequate natural light close to the perimeter but this will fall off dramatically towards the core of the building, five or six metres back from the glazing, and occupants will try to correct any deficiency by switching on the lights.

Various devices are now available to capture daylight and direct it deep into buildings and to reduce excessive light levels near glazing, providing a more uniform spread of natural light. Some of these, such as atria, light shelves, roof monitors or clerestorey lighting can have profound architectural design implications. Others such as prismatic glazing reflective blinds or shading systems can be more easily applied in the case of existing buildings. A wide range of specially-treated glazing materials which can control the intensity and optical properties of natural light and heat flows through windows is now available. [25,26,27]

The case for daylighting in buildings therefore has three strands: it can provide a healthier, more enjoyable indoor environment; it can conserve the earth's resources; and, because it saves energy it saves money.

COOLING STRATEGY

The following measures can help to avoid overheating:

- **Solar control:** to prevent the sun's rays from reaching, and in particular entering the building.
- **External gains control:** to prevent increases in heat due to conduction through the building skin or by the infiltration of external hot air.
- **Internal gains control:** to prevent unwanted heat from occupants and equipment raising internal temperatures.
- **Natural Cooling:** to transfer excess heat from the building to ambient heat sinks, including: ventilation, where unwanted hot air is replaced by fresh external air at a lower temperature.

SOLAR CONTROL

The most efficient way of protecting a building is to shade its windows and other apertures from unwanted direct sunlight. The degree and type of shade necessary depends on the position of the sun and the geometry of the building. [28]

Shading may be provided by vegetation, by adjacent buildings, or by fixed or moveable devices on the building. Deciduous vegetation can provide shade in summer and admit more light in winter. As the sun is fairly high in the sky in summer, south facing apertures receive less solar radiation and are easy to protect by horizontal overhangs which do not reduce solar gains in winter. Because the sun's altitude is low in the morning and evening, apertures facing east or west may require moveable vertical screens for effective shading without excessive loss of daylight.

Shutters, blinds, louvres, awnings and curtains are all examples of adjustable shading devices. Some can also be used in winter to increase thermal insulation. Ideally, shading devices should be placed on the exterior.

EXTERNAL GAINS CONTROL

External solar gains can be minimised by insulation, reduced window size, use of thermal inertia, reflection, or compact site layout. Warm air infiltration gains can be reduced by cooling the incoming air and by reducing infiltration. [29]

INTERNAL GAINS

Internal heat gains vary considerably, but for a typical household can be as follows:

Occupants	4.0 kWh/day
Lighting	1.5
Appliances & cooking	6.5
Hot water	3.0
Total	15.0

Efficient appliances and lighting can minimise these values, and appropriate ventilation design can reduce their effects on comfort in summer. [30]

NATURAL COOLING

Internal air speeds can be increased to maximise perceived cooling. Air adjacent to the building can be cooled by evaporation or shading. The temperature of ventilation air can be reduced by ground cooling, for example through buried pipes. The building fabric can be cooled by night-time radiative heat loss to the sky and by cross ventilation. [31]

Building occupants' perceptions of comfort are influenced by a number of parameters. Some of these such as air temperature, mean radiant temperature, relative humidity and air velocity relate to the environment. Others relate to the occupants and include, for instance, levels of activity, clothing and skin temperature.

Careful organisation of rooms according to their function can help keep the living spaces as cool as possible; for example by facing living areas north and using well-ventilated buffer spaces on the south side.

Evaporative Cooling

To change its state from liquid to vapour, water requires a certain amount of heat known as the latent heat of vaporisation. When this heat is supplied by hot air there is a drop in air temperature accompanied by an increase in humidity.

The evaporative cooling effect can be maximised by increasing both the air/water contact area and the relative movement of the air and water. Pools, fountains and water jets, etc., in adjacent outdoor spaces can cool ventilation air before it enters the building. Evaporative cooling cannot be used as effectively in humid climates where the air is already close to saturation. [32]

Radiative Heat Loss to the Sky

Because clear night skies are, even in the warm season, invariably cold, a significant amount of the heat which has accumulated in the building fabric during the day will be radiated to the sky, if the passage of heat from the building fabric is not impeded, for example, by insulation. Insulation may be needed to reduce heat losses in winter, or on warm days to inhibit the accumulation of heat in the building fabric. The design implications of movable insulation for walls and roofs are considerable. [33]

Ventilation for cooling:

Even when steps have been taken to shade a building, to reduce heat gains and to minimise the flow of external warm air into the building, internal temperatures in hot climates during summer can often be higher than those outside.

When external air is cooler than the upper comfort limit, fresh air driven through the building by naturally occurring differences in air pressure can help to remedy this problem. When two air masses have different temperatures, their densities and pressures are also different and this gives rise to movement of air from the denser (cooler) zone to the less dense (warmer) one. In situations where the air inside a building is warmer than ambient air and cooling is required, the temperature difference or 'stack' effect can be used to expel the warm air from the building. For example, by providing openings at the top and bottom of the building, warm air will rise naturally and escape from the top outlet while cooler fresh air will enter through the openings at the base. [34,35]

The rate of heat loss by convection from the building envelope can be accelerated by wind. This is particularly recommended for hot, humid climates. In hot, dry climates where night-time temperatures are low, cross ventilation at night is an appropriate method of removing heat accumulated in the building fabric during the day. [36]

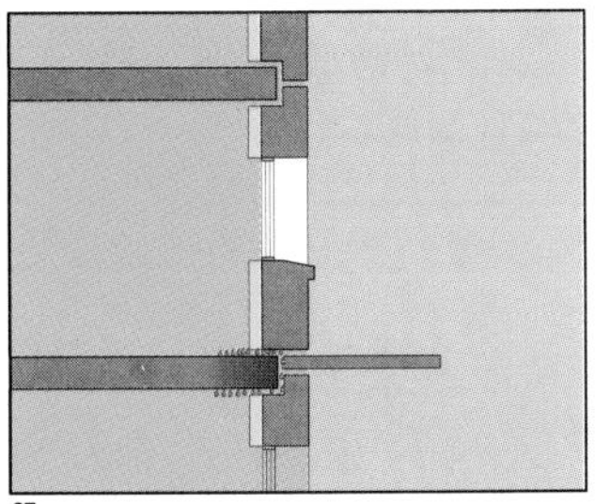
37

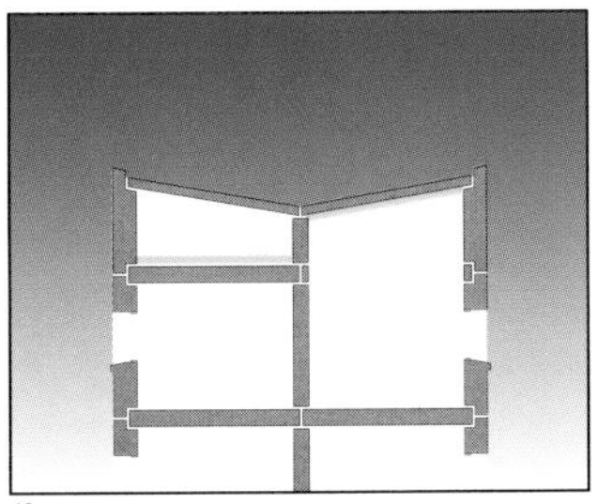
40

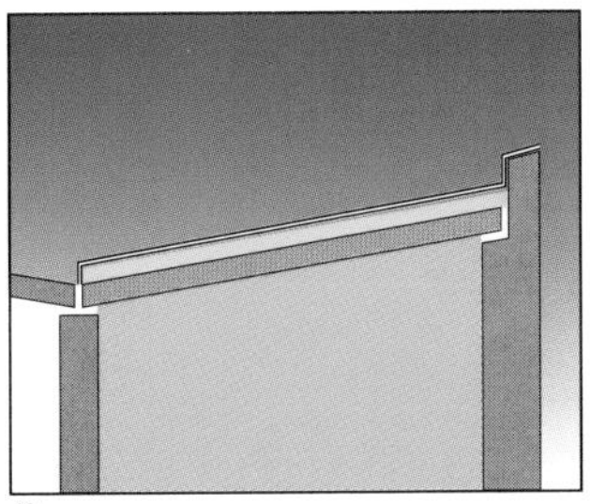
43

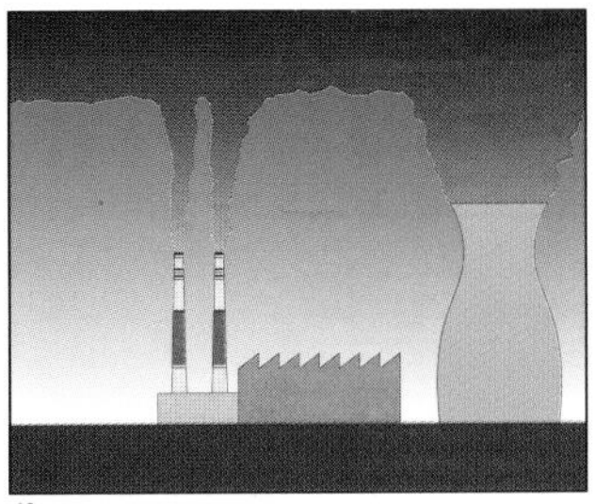
46

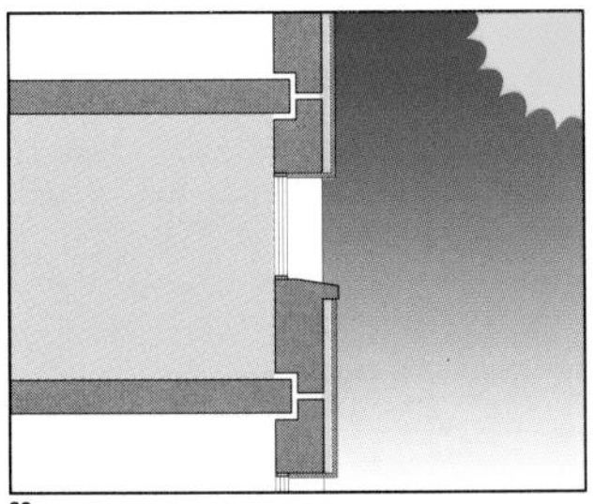
38

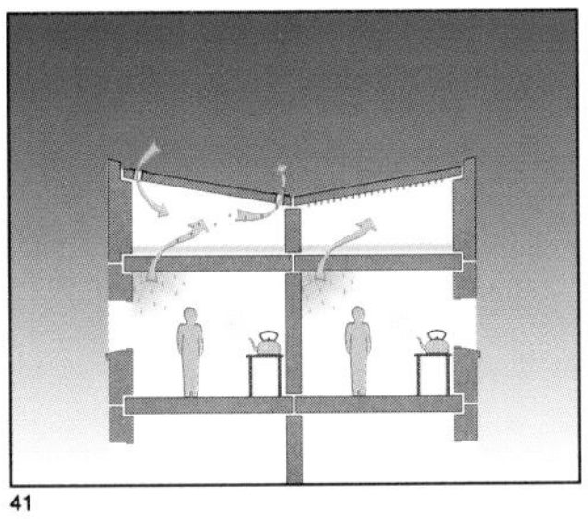
41

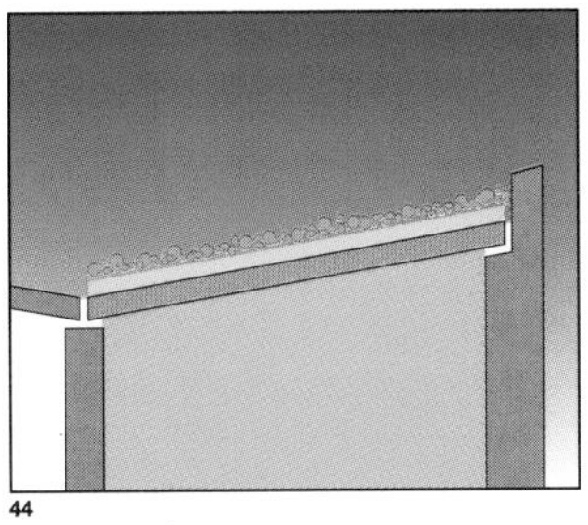
44

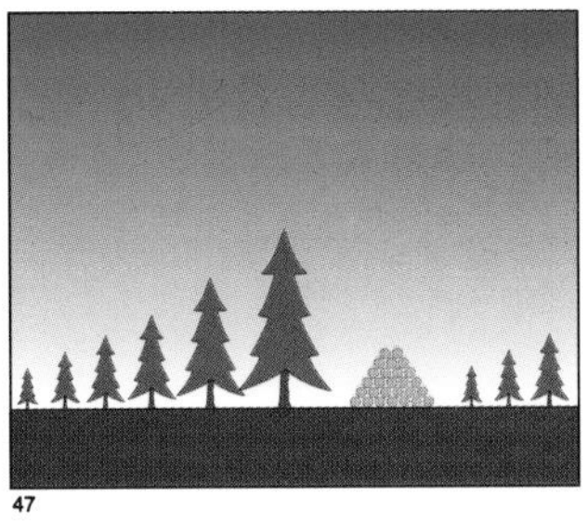
47

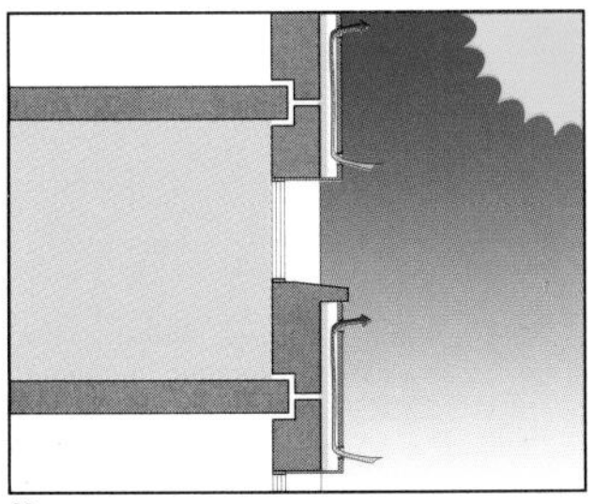
39

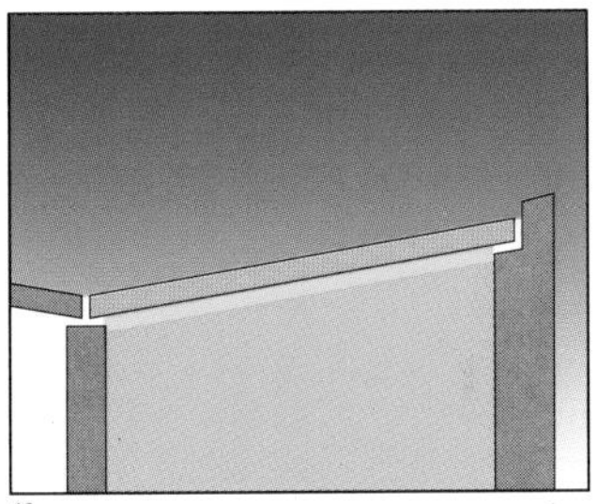
42

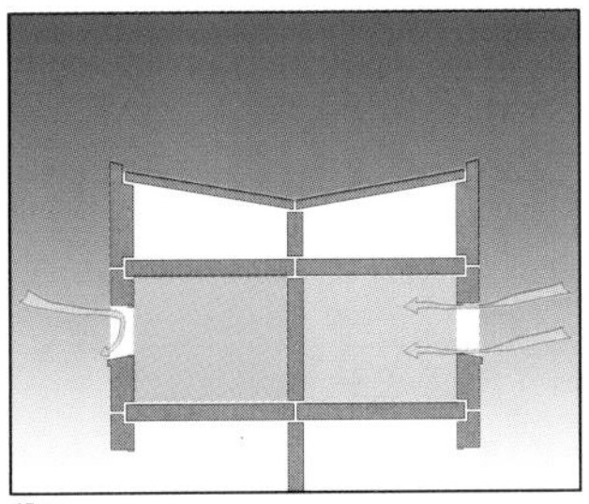
45

	MJ/tonne
Normal concrete	0.5
Precast concrete	1.4
Reinforced concrete	2.0
Chipboard panels	2.0
Bricks (light)	2.2
Bricks (heavy)	2.6
Precast reinforced concrete	2.9
Gypsum board	3.2
Mineral wool	18
Glass	22
Steel for reinforcement	26
Polystyrene foam	126
Aluminium sheets	261

Primary energy used in the materials and construction of buildings building (based on German data)

ENERGY CONSERVATION

By increasing the level of insulation and minimising heat losses due to ventilation during the heating season, and unwanted gains during warm weather, indoor comfort levels can be improved and the energy consumption of the building reduced considerably.

The correct design and placement of insulation is extremely important. It should be durable, continuous and have a thermal conductivity appropriate to the circumstances (climate, exposure etc.).

While it may be possible, and in some cases cheaper, to insulate internally, this reduces room sizes slightly, involves the replacement of skirtings, architraves and other items fixed to the wall and prevents the thermal mass of the building from storing heat. However, internally insulated rooms can be heated up more quickly which may be an advantage, for example where occupancy is intermittent. It is difficult, with internal insulation systems, to solve the problem of cold bridges which can lead to condensation and structural damage. [37]

Insulation may originally have been placed within the wall, roof or floor construction and if well fitted, it may still be effective; although certain insulations can deteriorate with age. However, it may be desirable to apply additional insulation to improve comfort and reduce energy use. In multi-storey buildings this will usually involve a choice of internal or external insulation systems.

External insulation combined with cladding or rendering systems, although sometimes initially more expensive, can: completely wrap the building with insulation, thus eliminating cold bridge problems; allow the thermal mass of the building to be used to moderate indoor temperature variations by acting as a heat store: improve the appearance and weather resistance of the building envelope; and result in lower maintenance costs. They also cause less inconvenience to occupants during installation, and where renovation of the facade and roof is necessary, the extra cost of the insulation system can often be recovered in about three years.

External wall insulation systems fall into three main categories:

The thin layer insulation or 'coat method'
Thin layer insulation is normally the cheapest option. Insulation, usually in the form of rigid panels, is fixed to the facade and a reinforced render or plaster coat of a special composition is applied to give a weather-proof external layer with a range of possible finishes. Care is needed in detailing and installing the render coat, especially around joints, corners, and window and door openings. Several proprietary systems exist. [38]

Ventilated facade insulation
The insulation is also fixed to the existing facade and the finishing panels are then installed using a spacer grid. The panels have openings which allow the outside air to ventilate the space between the panels and insulation. The advantages are greater breathability for the finished wall and better protection from the elements. In summer, the air flows through the void cooling the surface of the insulation thereby reducing heat gains through the wall. However, these air flows can also increase heat loss in winter if unrestricted. [39]

Pre-finished modules
Similar in thermal operation to ventilated facade insulation, the pre-finished modules arrive on site, ready for installation using special fixing systems which simplify the mounting operation and help to ensure a good quality of workmanship. The result is an external surface which doesn't require any further work.

ROOFS

Fitting roof insulation is often relatively easy and pay-back periods are short, as heat losses from roofs can be very large due to night-time radiation to the sky and the relatively large area of the roof. Care is necessary to control water vapour and condensation, by appropriate use of vapour barriers and ventilation. [40,41]

- Pitched roof loft insulation is an easy, low-cost action where insulation material, usually fibreglass quilt, mineral wool or rigid foam plastic panels, is placed horizontally either between timber joists or on top of a structural slab. It is often advisable to protect the insulation by, for example a wooden floor covering.

- To maintain and improve the use of the loft, insulation may be fitted to the pitched roof either inside the roof construction if access is easy, or in the case of tiles, outside the roof construction, immediately beneath the tiles. Typically the insulation is covered by internal cladding such as plasterboard or timber sheeting. External application is advisable if the roof needs to be repaired. In that case, specially formed panels may be applied to the joists, and the previously removed tiles replaced.

- There are three main methods of insulating flat roofs: With the *warm deck* the insulation is applied on the roof (which may have a defective finish) and is covered with a new waterproof layer, so that the roof construction remains within the heated volume. With the *cold deck* method, insulation is placed beneath the ceiling, so the roof construction remains outside the heated volume. In an *inverted roof*, ballasted water-resistant insulation is added above a suitable roof finish. [42,43,44]

IMPROVEMENTS TO WINDOWS

The more layers of air trapped between glass panes, the lower the heat loss through the window. For example, in a window of 1.5 m² area and an outside temperature of minus 5°C, the heat loss with single glazing will be 195 W while if it is triple glazed this will reduce to 75 W. During winter, the inner surface of a multi-glazed window is warmer thus improving comfort and reducing or eliminating condensation. It is often possible to fit secondary glazing on existing frames with only minor adaptations. Several advanced types of glazing are now available which can dramatically improve the energy performance of the window. One of the more common of these, low emissivity glazing, incorporates a pane of specially coated glass which admits the full radiation spectrum, including short wave radiation, but inhibits long wave radiation from the room. Additionally, the cavities between glass panes in double or triple glazed units can be filled with a heavy gas such as argon which resists convective movement in the cavity thus reducing heat loss further.

Other, currently expensive types of advanced glazing systems include transparent insulation materials (TIM), which provide high levels of thermal insulation and relatively high levels of diffuse light transmission and solar gain. They may be in the form of semitransparent aerogels, polycarbonate honeycomb or polymethylmethacrylate capillary structures contained within glazing panels. These TIM materials can be used to cover mass walls where they admit solar radiation during the day and insulate the wall at night. Shading may be necessary to prevent overheating in summer, even at northern latitudes.

In general, but particularly in windy areas, the poor air-tightness of window and external door frames results in heat loss from indoors. Draught stripping can help, but where frames are seriously damaged or aged, they should be changed for new well-sealed ones. [45]

SELECTION OF MATERIALS

Careful, informed selection of materials and components used in buildings can improve environmental conditions indoors, and can have a significant, cumulative effect on the health of the environment. The objective is to select construction materials which have the least practicable embodied energy content, or to minimise the energy consumed in their extraction, manufacture and delivery to the building site; and which, during their manufacture, useful life and disposal have the least possible damaging effects on the environment. The potential for re-cycling used materials is important.

Embodied energy can give an indication of the likely environmental damage caused by the production of greenhouse gasses and other pollutants, in particular CO_2, SO_2, CFCs and NOx. The depletion of non-renewable resources such as fossil fuels, some timbers and rare materials is also an issue of some concern.

The evaluation and selection of the least environmentally damaging materials is not a simple matter. For example, the manufacture of a brick made in a factory using an oil fired kiln will have a significantly greater environmental impact than a similar brick from a factory supplied by hydro-electric power. Comparisons should ideally be made with a knowledge of the environmental effects of extraction of raw materials, such as whether they come from a sustainable source and what are the local and global effects (pollution of watercourses and land, erosion of soils and consequent flooding, social disruption etc.). We should know what are the energy and environmental effects of manufacture. When installed in buildings, many materials can continue to have an environmental impact, for example by the emission of harmful substances: as gasses from paints or preservatives, and from plastics used for insulation or in furnishings; or as dust particles from such materials as asbestos. Finally, it is important to compare the embodied energy of a material with its potential for energy saving during its useful life, for example insulation. [46,47]

Some general guidelines may be followed:

1 Use materials that require low energy input during extraction, manufacture, transport, construction, use, demolition and disposal. Where a high energy content material must be used, ensure that it is used in its most efficient form and that it can be recycled.

2 Use materials in a form that can be easily reclaimed and re-used with a minimum of re-processing. Avoid the use of composite materials which make separation for re-cycling difficult.

3 Use materials with minimal impact on the environment throughout their life-cycles, especially atmospheric pollution. Use materials from sustainable sources in preference to non-renewable ones, and re-cycled materials in preference to new ones.

4 Maximise the design life of a building, ensuring that elements with shorter design lives can be easily replaced and maintained:

Element	Typical design life (years)	Number of cycles in 100 years
structure	100	1
services	25	4
finishes	5	20

5 Request detailed information from manufacturers on the energy content of their products as well as their environmental impacts during manufacture and use.

The list above gives only a rough indication of the environmental impact of some construction materials. The amount of embodied energy will vary according to manufacturing efficiency, fuel type, and the procurement of raw materials. When specifying construction materials, such figures should also be interpreted with regard to the relative quantities of the materials used in the building and their life-cycle environmental impacts. For example, aluminium might only be used in small quantities as a vapour barrier; and foam plastic or glass-fibre used as insulation may save many times more energy in use than consumed in its manufacture.

ARCHITECTS

ARCHITECTS

1 ST PRIZE ARCHITECTS – 26A

Amilcar Dos Santos, Frank Le Bail and Jean-François Perretant of Novae Architects, Lyon, France

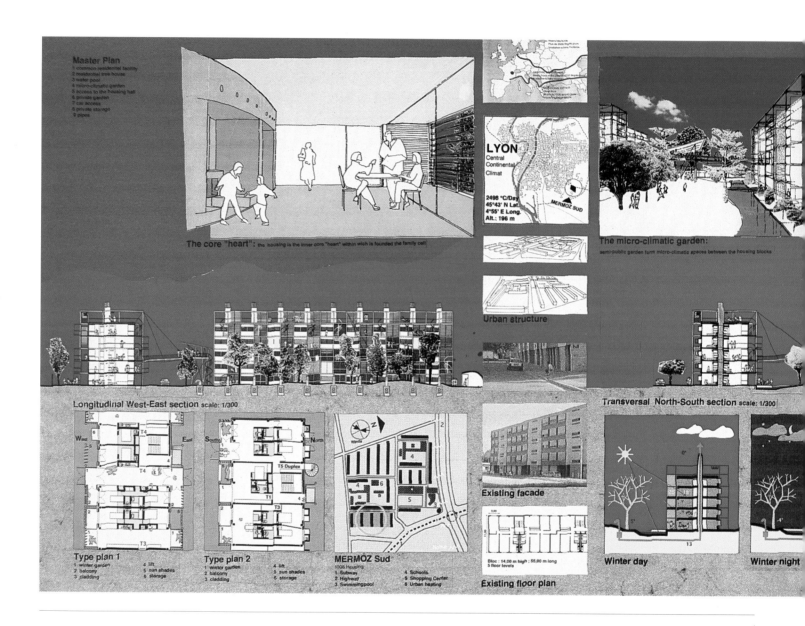

BIOGRAPHIES

AMILCAR DOS SANTOS
Dipl. Architecture École d'Architecture de Lyon, 1983. Project architect for the École d'Architecture de Lyon which won the 'Equerre d'Argent' for Jourda-Perraudin in 1987. Associate Architect with Novae Architects in Lyon since 1994, and Associate Professor in the École d'Architecture de Lyon.

FRANK LE BAIL
Dipl. Architecture, École d'Architecture de San Etienne, 1986. Worked with Diaz-Le Bail, 1988-92, and with Le Bail in 1993. Associate Architect in Novae Architects since 1994. Has received many special mentions in competitions with Dos Santos and Perretant.

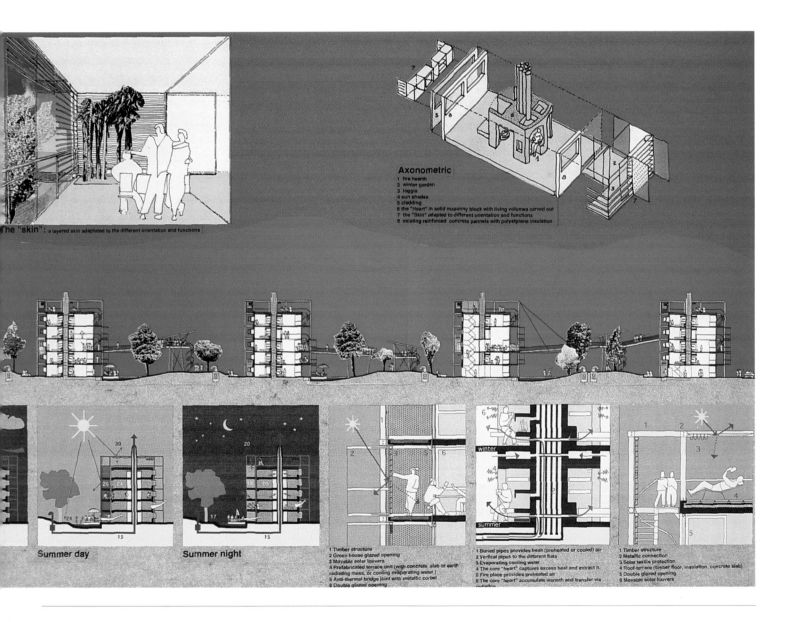

PROJECT DESCRIPTION

JEAN-FRANÇOIS PERRETANT
Dipl. Architecture École d'Architecture de Lyon, 1985. Project
Director with Jourda-Perraudin,
1987-93. Associate Architect
with Novae Architects in Lyon,
1994, and Associate Professor
in the École d'Architecture de
Lyon and in the Université
Lyon, 1995-96.

This project entitled the 'Heart
and the Skin' is located in Mermoz Suz, Lyon, and comprises
18 blocks of apartments.
The 'heart' is the core, warmed
in winter by preheated fresh air
and cooled in summer by fresh
air via underground pipes and
excess heat extracted via ventilation ducts to the exterior.
The skin is the buffer zone,

adapted to the different orientations and functions of apartments providing winter garden,
veranda, loggia, storage,
clothes drying etc.
The apartments have dual orientation, providing natural
cross ventilation and sun or
shade.
The large communal gardens
between the blocks form mi-

cro-climatic spaces with vegetation and water basins providing water cooling in summer
and reflecting sun and light in
winter.
The 'tree houses' accommodate communal activities,
meetings, music and games in
summer which would normally
take place indoors in winter.
Apartments at ground level

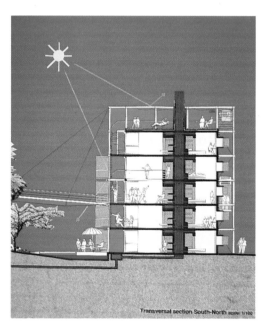

Transversal section South-North scale 1/100

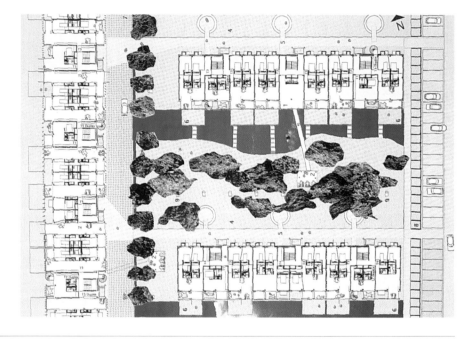

TECHNICAL ASSESSMENT

have small private terraces, and upper level apartments have access to rooftop terraces. Intervention has been limited to three areas: the 'heart', updating the services; the 'skin', with insulation and weatherproofing; and the landscape. It represents a solution of an intermediate level of intervention, but may be expensive to build and

has limited potential for replication. The treatment of the ventilation ducts is unsatisfactory; however the project addressed most of the issues in a convincing and comprehensive manner of good architectural quality.

This scheme adopted an interesting strategy – the provision of a massive core to provide thermal stability, surrounding it with a lightweight envelope providing solar gain in winter, daylight and natural ventilation. The architect referred to this as the "heart" and the "skin" and as a concept it appealed to the assessors as an appropriate re-

sponse. The heart becomes a "hearth" in its function of winter heating and is realised as a massive masonry construction actually incorporating an open fire. This massive structure also functions to temper the incoming fresh air. In summer the hearth structure reverses its function to provide a 'coolth' store, cooled by air from buried

pipes, and further cooled by evaporative cooling as the air emerges into the room; although the assessors had reservations concerning the effectiveness of this latter system.

Shading correctly responds to orientation and is supported on a secondary frame structure. This permits a highly respon-sive shading system, although the assessors felt that ade-quate shading might have been provided much more economi-cally.

The architects anticipated a "nomadic" use of the building - using the full area of the enve-lope in summer and retreating to the hearth in winter. This seems to be a little dramatic for a mild climate such as Lyon, and anticipates a reduction in useable space in an already minimally-sized accommoda-tion. It might have been better to concentrate resources on in-sulating the envelope to a high standard, thereby including the maximum space at acceptable comfort conditions. Further-more, the servicing function of the massive core would carry many technical problems and require a considerable invest-ment for a modest improve-ment in energy performance.

2 ND PRIZE ARCHITECTS – 39A

Sandrine Jourdain and Olivier Molla, Vitry sur Seine, France

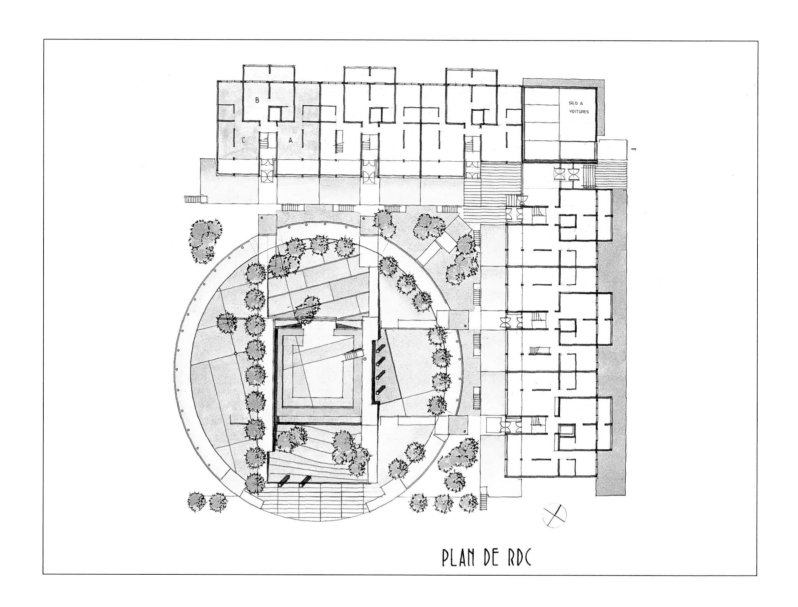

PLAN DE RDC

BIOGRAPHIES

SANDRINE JOURDAIN
Diplomé de l'École d'Architecture de Paris Conflans, 1994. Student work exhibited in Morocco, Greece, the Netherlands and San Francisco. Awarded lauréat in competition d'Art Urbain Robert Auzelle, 1994.

OLIVIER MOLLA
Diplomé de l'École d'Architecture de Paris Conflans, 1994. Mention in Grand Prix d'Architecture de l'Institute de France, 1992. Student work exhibited in Spain, the Netherlands, Greece and Egypt. Military service in l'Arme du Genie as an architect 1994-95. Statut d'Architecture Liberale 1995.

PROJECT DESCRIPTION

This project on the Pécs site in Hungary has concentrated on improving the internal and external spaces and aims to improve comfort conditions both inside and out.

It offers a considerable improvent of the internal spaces, with excellent spatial integration. A mixture of apartment sizes has been achieved includ-

FACADE SUD et OUEST

ing duplex apartments.

Buffer spaces on the south and west facades offer a larger living space with moveable panels replacing the double height existing wall. The buffer space with glazed sliding screens and the partially glazed moveable screens offer flexibility for seasonal changes. The buffer space also allows enhanced daylight.

No buffer spaces are provided on the top floor, but it is clad similarly to north and east facades with polished concrete panels fixed to a metal structure and insulated. Lifts have been provided.

A multi-storey carpark has been constructed to enclose the north-east corner of the apartment buildings, providing sixty-eight car spaces and a thermal buffer on the gable walls. The open space formally used for carparking has been transformed into a garden for communal use. Ground floor apartments have small, private gardens which form buffer spaces to the communal garden.

The quality and sensitivity of presentation reflect the quality of the design of this project on the Pécs site.

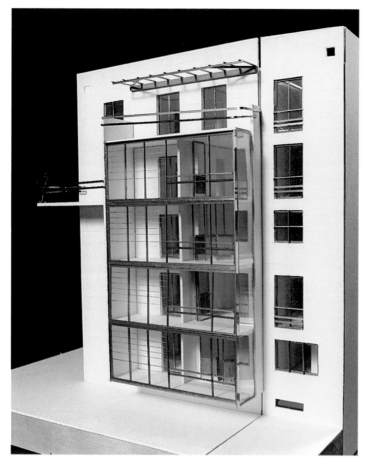

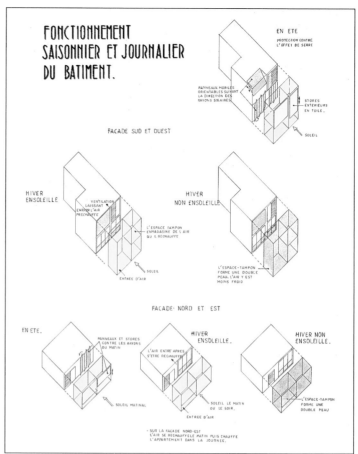

FONCTIONNEMENT SAISONNIER ET JOURNALIER DU BATIMENT.

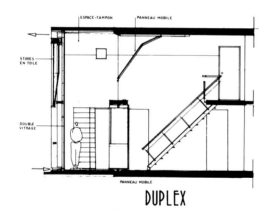

DUPLEX

LOGEMENT SIMPLE – 44 m 2

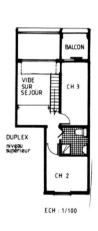

ECH : 1/100

TECHNICAL ASSESSMENT

This scheme relies on the application of buffer-spaces together with extra insulation. The buffer-spaces are shown to respond to both orientation and season, recognising the need to admit or reject solar gains when available. The double storey height wall separating the interior from the buffer-space is replaced by moveable panels which respond to solar geometry, providing varying degrees of coupling between the bufferspace and the interior.

The strategy was considered sound, although there was some concern by the technical assessors at the lack of technical detail on the structure of the additional buffer-spaces, and how the opening up of the separating wall could be achieved without threatening the integrity of the structure.

The assessors also queried if the addition of two buffer spaces to one apartment was an over-provision, given that this also could interfere with cross-ventilation, daylighting and views from the interior spaces.

Very high energy saving were predicted from the LT4 analysis, although the assessors had some doubts about the validity of this. It seemed notable also, that whilst assuming that the initial system efficiency was only 40%, no mention was made of improving this.

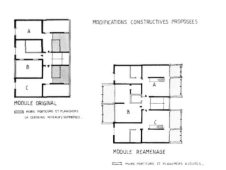

MODIFICATIONS CONSTRUCTIVES PROPOSEES

MODULE ORIGINAL

MURS PORTEURS ET PLANCHERS
(A CERTAINS NIVEAUX) SUPPRIMES.

MODULE REAMENAGE

MURS PORTEURS ET PLANCHERS AJOUTES.

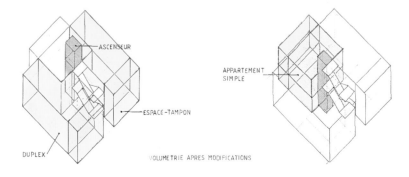

ASCENSEUR

ESPACE-TAMPON

DUPLEX

APPARTEMENT
SIMPLE

VOLUMETRIE APRES MODIFICATIONS

3RD PRIZE ARCHITECTS – 102A
Harri Hagan, Helsinki, Finland

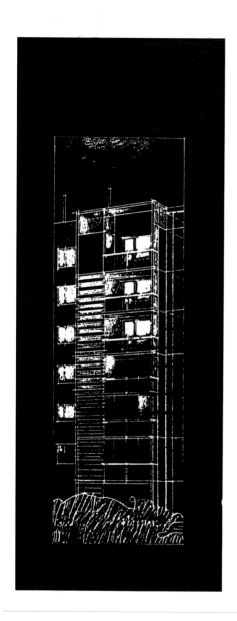

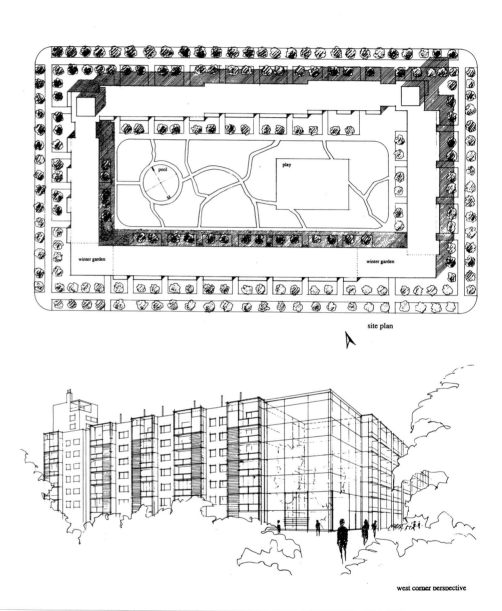

site plan

west corner perspective

PROJECT DESCRIPTION

This project on the Marzhan site in Berlin provides a solution which does not involve major destruction of the existing fabric of the building. The enclosure of the open corners by the addition of winter gardens to the south and apartments and services to the north provides a private communal open space with an enhanced microcli-mate. Wintergardens provide communal indoor spaces with heat recovery and cooling systems for the entire block of apartments. Balconies are upgraded with a steel structure with sliding glazed and timber panels and black stone and timber flooring to provide a sheltered dining space. Kitchens are opened up. Staircases are opened up and a lift provided. Cladding panels to the north and east are to be upgraded with insulation and warm air collectors.

The project is a low-key but elegant solution, and treats the building in a light, fine manner.

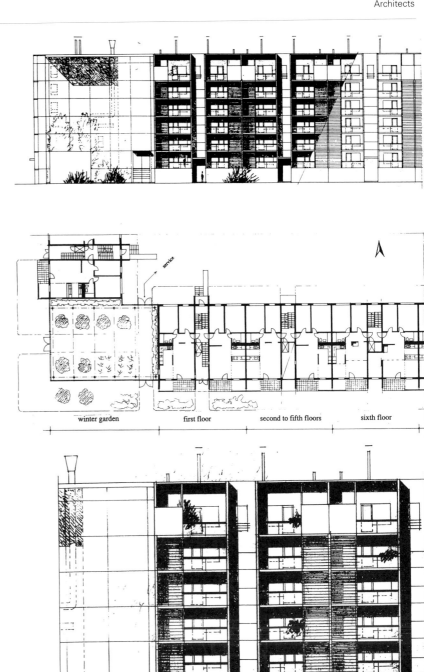

winter garden   first floor   second to fifth floors   sixth floor

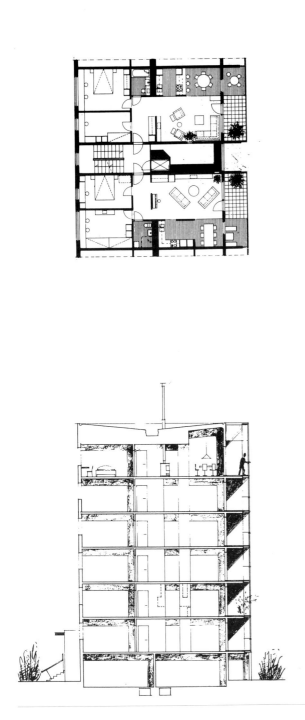

TECHNICAL ASSESSMENT

The closing of the square with the winter garden certainly would improve winter conditions. It might be argued that there would be a penalty of reduced breezes in summer, although in the northerly region of Europe this is of lower priority. Wintergardens, or atria, require careful control with shading and ventilation. No details of this were given.

The glazing and shading of the existing balconies would improve their own environment and lead to energy saving for the building as a whole. But there is little detail about how they would operate. For example, are they to be used as ventilation pre-heat sources? What happens to the separating wall?

The architects proposed to clad the building in "poor man's solar collector" consisting of 50mm of applied insulation with a dark external facing surface. A 25mm air gap separated this from an external layer of 6mm opal glass. The solar heated air from this void is then allowed to enter the building via the window frames. This is a sound strategy, even if carrying certain technical problems. For example, without shading, the collector surface will become very hot in summer. What happens to that hot air which it generates?

Overall the assessors felt that although it suggested plausible strategies, there was a lack of technical detail.

4TH PRIZE ARCHITECTS – 44A
Félix Jové Sandoval and José María Jové Sandoval, Valladolid, Spain

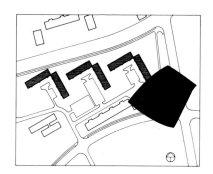

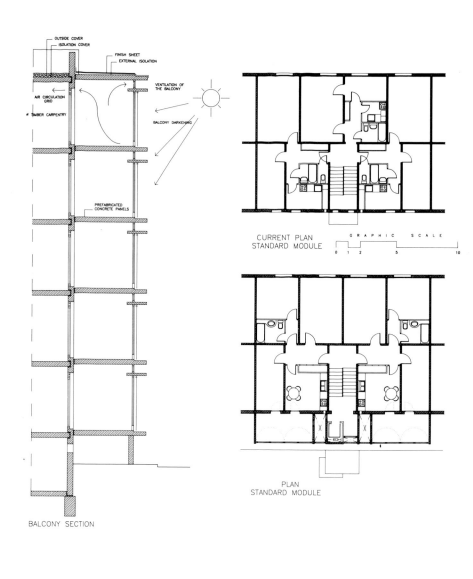

CURRENT PLAN
STANDARD MODULE

GRAPHIC SCALE

PLAN
STANDARD MODULE

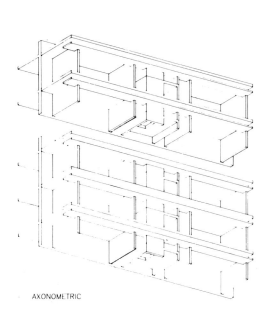

AXONOMETRIC

BALCONY SECTION

PROJECT DESCRIPTION

This project on the Pécs site is a prime example of low-key intervention which achieves a significant level of improvement at a modest cost and has good potential for replication. It is a design solution, that with a few changes could be suitable to many different situations. It provides a balcony giving access space, solving problems found in many apartment buildings of this age. The balcony provides a sunny outdoor space in summer and with glazed panels closed in winter, collects and distributes heat to the rooms inside. Space is also available for a lift. A reorganisation of the internal space distributing the smallest apartment equally to the two larger ones, with three apartments becoming two, without construction changes. The design has been executed in a clear and simple manner, but could be improved by further development.

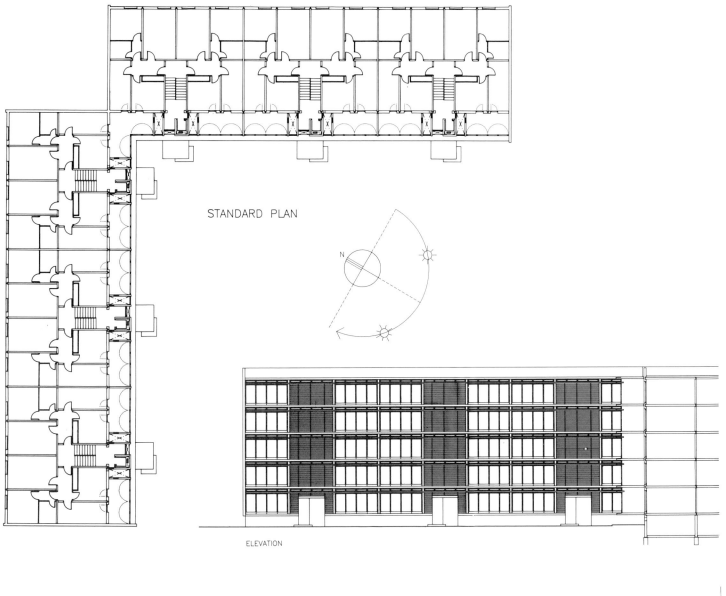

STANDARD PLAN

ELEVATION

CURRENT STANDARD PLAN   CURRENT ELEVATION

TECHNICAL ASSESSMENT

The aims of this scheme, to produce a general solution for a common apartment type, involving both improved energy efficiency and space standards, was laudable. Space standards were improved by the transformation of three apartments into two, but since the southerly facades were occupied by kitchens and lift shafts, it has to be asked if this was the best rearrangement of accommodation. Details of how the energy saving was to be achieved were severely lacking, and certain technical problems such as external insulation were not addressed at all. The shading of the balconies was incorrectly dealt with due to errors in representing solar angles on the SE facade. No energy analysis, comfort analysis, nor discussion of expected results was given.

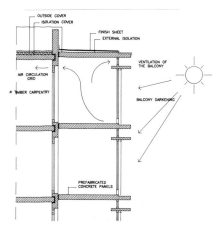

4TH PRIZE ARCHITECTS – 38A
Pierre Drolez and Elisabeth Lemercier, Paris, France

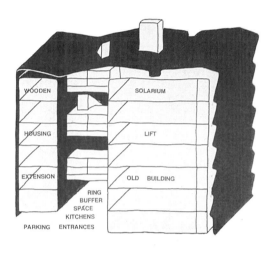

VIEW FROM THE KITCHEN

NORTHERN

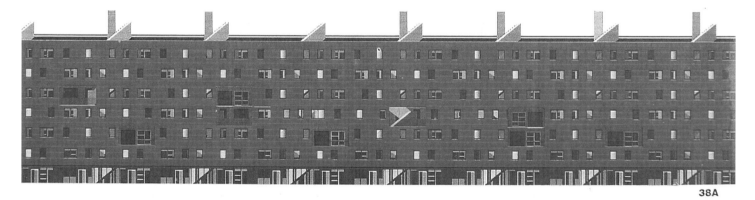

38A

PROJECT DESCRIPTION

This project on the Marzhan site in Berlin takes a completely opposite approach to the other joint fourth prizewinner; they illustrate two radically different approaches to the same problem. The approach in this scheme is to construct a structure parallel to the existing, to the north and west a timber structure and to the south and east a sunspace, a fully glazed skin. The timber structure provides a variety of accomodation which can be utilised independently or linked to the existing by the staircase which has a glazed roof.

While of significant architectural quality, it is not thoroughly developed in terms of energy and environmental issues.

TECHNICAL ASSESSMENT

This scheme constructs a new parallel service terrace of wood on the N and W sides linked by bridges and roofed over to the main building with glazing. A fully glazed skin to the S and E facades is proposed.

The technical assessors were very doubtful of both these strategies. The first would cause a serious degradation to

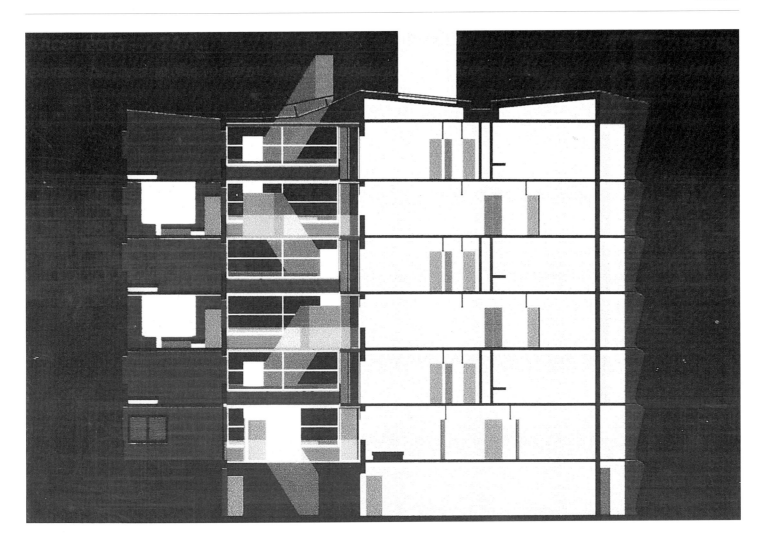

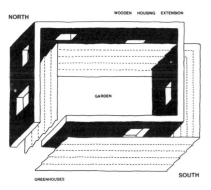

NORTH

WOODEN HOUSING EXTENSION

GARDEN

GREENHOUSES

SOUTH

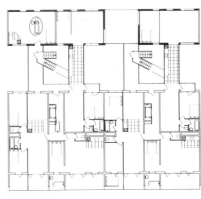

the views, daylighting and natural ventilation of the N and W facing spaces in the original part of the building (in effect turning it into a very deep plan building). No comment is made by the architects on how this space would be ventilated and what its insulating effect on the original building would be. The second strategy is technically difficult and expensive, for relatively modest returns in energy saving compared with a sensible insulation strategy. It would also generate severe overheating problems for which shading and ventilation does not seem to have been considered.

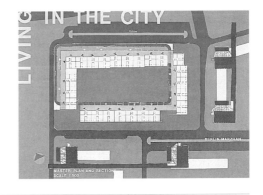

LIVING IN THE CITY

BERLIN-MARZHAN

MASTER PLAN AND SECTION
SCALE 1:500

COMMENDED ARCHITECTS – 95A
Rob Marsh, Büro-E, Copenhagen, Denmark

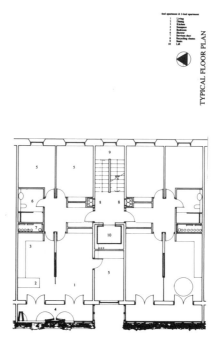

TYPICAL FLOOR PLAN

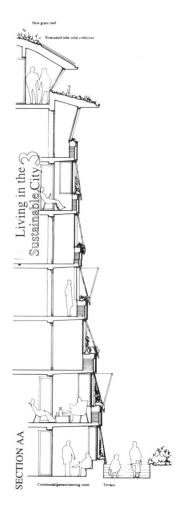

Living in the Sustainable City 3

SECTION AA

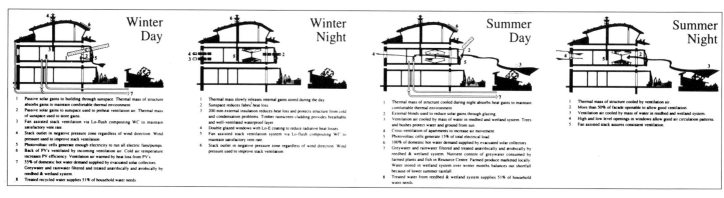

Winter Day   Winter Night   Summer Day   Summer Night

PROJECT DESCRIPTION

This project on the Marzhan site in Berlin addresses the energy and environmental issues in a convincing manner and is sensitive in its use of materials, its ecological image and good energy performance. A lightweight timber structure has created top floor apartments with a grass-covered roof with integrated solar collectors.

TECHNICAL ASSESSMENT

This was the highest rated scheme by the technical assessors. It is the only scheme that addresses the whole range of issues raised in the brief, from improved social conditions to environmental sustainability. It showed a well-integrated and comprehensive approach, although in presentation the architecture tended to become eclipsed by the analysis.

The walls and roof were insulated to a U-value of 0.2, appropriate for the northerly Continental site. Sunspaces were added and the role of thermal mass and shading properly considered.

Low-E glazing was installed in all windows with the N-facing glazing being reduced and the S-facing area being increased. Very high energy savings were predicted with the LT method. In reality this would not be the case (it is using LT beyond its normal working limits) and it would have been useful to have had some discussion on this.

E XHIBITED ARCHITECTS – 5A
Studio E Architects Limited, London, United Kingdom

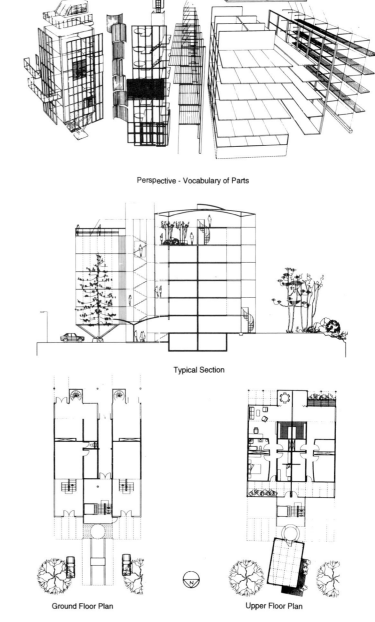

Perspective - Vocabulary of Parts

Typical Section

Ground Floor Plan

Upper Floor Plan

PROJECT DESCRIPTION

This project for a five storey building at Ursynow, Warsaw, strips the building of non-structural facade, roof and internal elements, and in replacing them provides more accomodation to each apartment in an envelope of higher specification. Both facades have been extended with balconies of open or enclosed design, and all extended living spaces overlook gardens. A new circulation core, outside the existing building, accomodates lift and stairs and a proposed studio flat, which can be of flexible orientation. The street level apartments have been proposed as home business areas while the existing basement level is retained for plant and storage.

Penthouse apartments are added.

While this project has upgraded the building in a successful manner, significant demolition of the existing building and major reconstruction is costly and could not be replicated in many situations.

TECHNICAL ASSESSMENT

A very thorough and logical analysis has been provided for this scheme which relies upon a major intervention to the existing structure. However the realisation of the design does not come through clearly and the presentation lacks detail in shading design and ventilation provision.

E XHIBITED ARCHITECTS – 21A
Héléne Mehats Grutter and Alexandre Grutter, Strasbourg, France

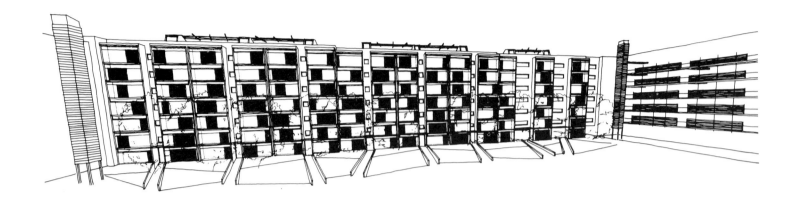

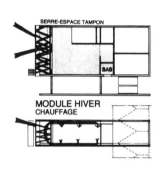

MODULE HIVER
CHAUFFAGE

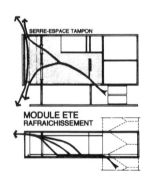

MODULE ETE
RAFRAICHISSEMENT

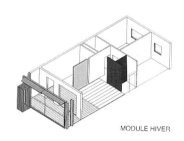

MODULE HIVER

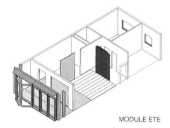

MODULE ETE

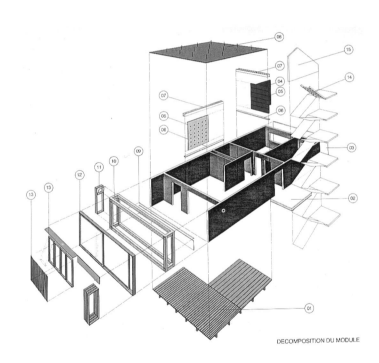

DECOMPOSITION DU MODULE

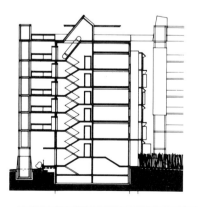

PROJECT DESCRIPTION

This project on the Berlin site has significicant intervention at two levels, to the building and the site. Daytime spaces are located to the south with nightime spaces to the north. Buffer spaces are provided to the living / daytime areas, with sliding glazed screens, sliding and tilting timber venetian blinds and internal shutters, all controlled by the occupant to facilitate the use of the space in all seasons. The stairs have been enlarged to accomodate a lift and to give access to the roof level sunspace and garden. The communal garden at ground level contains planting, ponds, and sunspaces for outdoor activities with ground level occupants having a private garden.

TECHNICAL ASSESSMENT

Realistic proposal, if not particularly innovative. Thermal performance and comfort good. Ventilation well considered. Good potential for replication, little disturbance to occupants during construction. Good presentation of ideas.

E XHIBITED ARCHITECTS – 55A
Roberto Grio, Rome, Italy

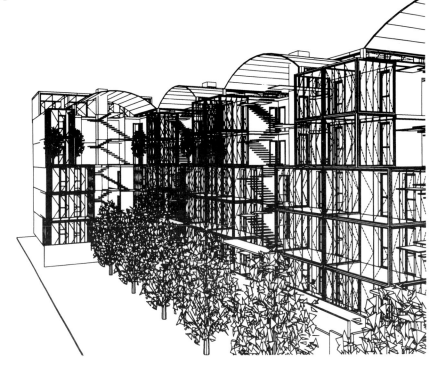

ENERGETIC BEHAVIOUR OF THE NEW FACADE SYSTEM

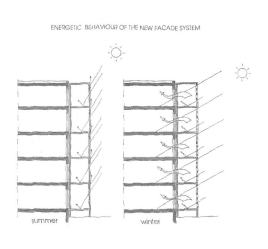

summer   winter

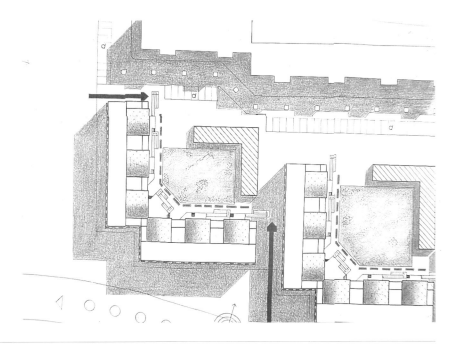

PROJECT DESCRIPTION

This project on the Pécs site has set out as its basic theme to enclose the courtyard and to ensure that the living rooms open to the courtyard. The first, second and third floor apartments are single level with living spaces opening to the sunspaces (which are totally glazed or open according to season). By removing the stairs from its original position, replaced by a lift and duplex apartments on the fourth and fifth floors, an atrium has been achieved. Constructed with a steel frame and covered by a semi-transparent vault, terraces are formed with planting and sunspaces. The areas not covered by the vault at roof level are for communal activities.

TECHNICAL ASSESSMENT

Interesting architectural solution but not a comprehensive solution of the problems. However, the overall concept is convincing though the constructive details have not been developed in depth. Relatively expensive rehabilitation that may be feasible if situated in the right area.

E XHIBITED ARCHITECTS – 106A
Wojciech Korbel, Cracow, Poland

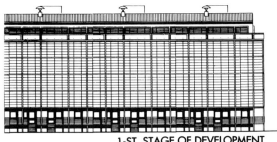

1-ST STAGE OF DEVELOPMENT

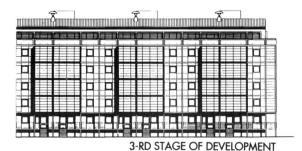

3-RD STAGE OF DEVELOPMENT

SECTION B-B

W E

A- EXISTING BUILDING
B- 3-RD STAGE BALCONY
    -THERMAL BUFFER
C- 2-ND STAGE BALCONY
    -THERMAL BUFFER OR A SPACE
    FOR APARTMENT EXTENSION
D- TOP FLOOR -THERMAL BUFFER
E- ADDITIONAL NEW CLADDING

LOSS OF HEAT PROTECTION DIAGRAM

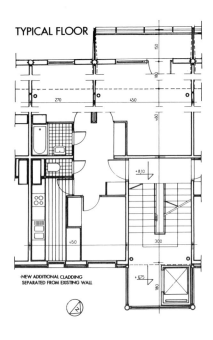

TYPICAL FLOOR

-NEW ADDITIONAL CLADDING
SEPARATED FROM EXISTING WALL

1-ST STAGE OF DEVELOPMENT

A
PRESENT CONDITION

C
NEW TOP FLOOR /ART STUDIOS/

2-ND STAGE OF DEVELOPMENT

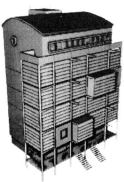

INDIVID. PARTICIPATION
ALLOWS THE APARTMENT EXTENSION

3-RD STAGE OF DEVELOPMENT

ALL THE APARTMENTS EXTENDED

PROJECT DESCRIPTION

This project on two similar buildings in Cracow built in 1972, has proposed retrofitting the building in phases, to provide for the possibility of improvements by the occupier. On the west facade a structure is established to create balconies with additional structure to allow for the apartments to be extended at alater stage.

When the balconies are in place, a glazing system can be installed or the apartment can be extended and the glazed area added.

The east facade is to be insulated, new windows installed and the staircases extended to provide space for a lift. An extra floor has been added to include art studios.

TECHNICAL ASSESSMENT

A three-stage refurbishment with elaboration of the west facade with extensions and conservatories but no shading provided. The overheating calculations are not carried out. External insulation is left as an option, yet no mention of the heating system or ventilation is made.

E XHIBITED ARCHITECTS – 46A

Judith Ubarrechena, L2M Architects, San Sebastian, Spain

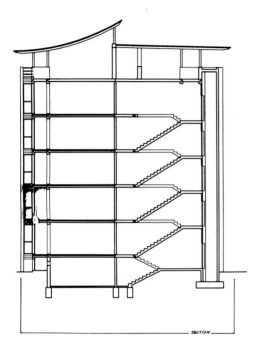

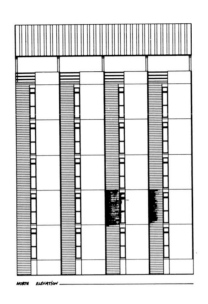

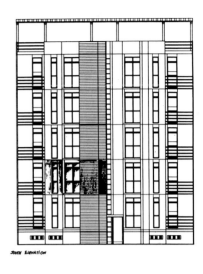

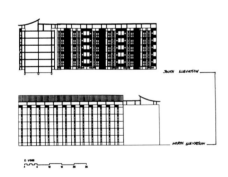

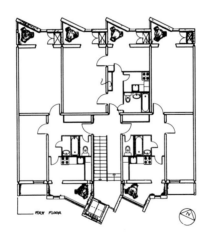

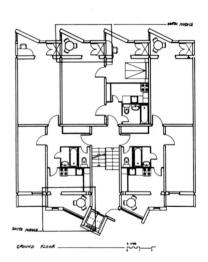

PROJECT DESCRIPTION

This project on the Pécs site involves minimum intervention to the existing building providing a 'skin' to the north and south facades. This skin takes the form of a glazed space to the south and a concrete panelled space to the north. A lift is provided in the entrance area on the south facade. The spaces on the south facade collect and store heat and include shading devices. A solid west facade is proposed to avoid overheating. A new curved roof provides protection for the existing structure and promotes ventilation for cooling in summer.

TECHNICAL ASSESSMENT

Thoughtful analysis identifying modest solutions to key problems but the design needs further development. Serious concern about daylighting and ventilation was expressed by the Technical Assessors, but this project could represent a replicable solution.

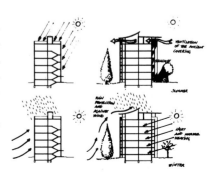

E XHIBITED ARCHITECTS – 124A

Dimitris Polychronopoulos, Matina Georgopoulou and George Kontoroupis
Athens, Greece

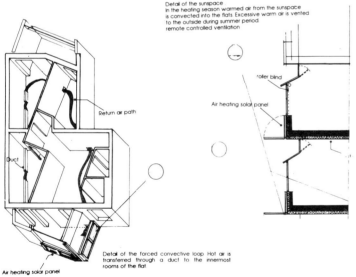

Detail of the sunspace
In the heating season warmed air from the sunspace is convected into the flats. Excessive warm air is vented to the outside during summer period.
remote controlled ventilation

Return air path

Air heating solar panel

roller blind

Duct

Detail of the forced convective loop Hot air is transferred through a duct to the innermost rooms of the flat

Air heating solar panel

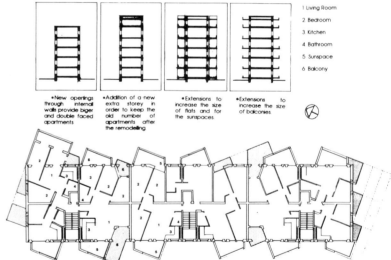

1 Living Room
2 Bedroom
3 Kitchen
4 Bathroom
5 Sunspace
6 Balcony

• New openings through internal walls provide bigger and double faced apartments

• Addition of a new extra storey in order to keep the old number of apartments after the remodelling.

• Extensions to increase the size of flats and for the sunspaces.

• Extensions to increase the size of balconies.

PROJECT DESCRIPTION

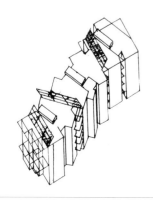

In this project on the Moscow site where buildings are orientated east west, the addition of sunspaces orientated directly or within forty five degrees of south is proposed. The extensions, in the form of independent metal structures, increase the size of the re-planned apartments, with most apartments having two sunspaces. Internal roller blinds provide shade. Solar panels are located on the parapet of each sunspace. The addition of a top storey replaces the apartments lost through replanning. External insulation and double glazing are provided.

TECHNICAL ASSESSMENT

The addition of south / south-east / south-west facing balconies to buildings of this orientation is innovative. Internal re-planning is questionable. Good consideration has been given to winter and summer conditions, but the proposed ventilation strategy may be unrealistic. No consideration of external spaces is evident.

EXHIBITED ARCHITECTS – 33A
Andrew Holmes, Paris, France

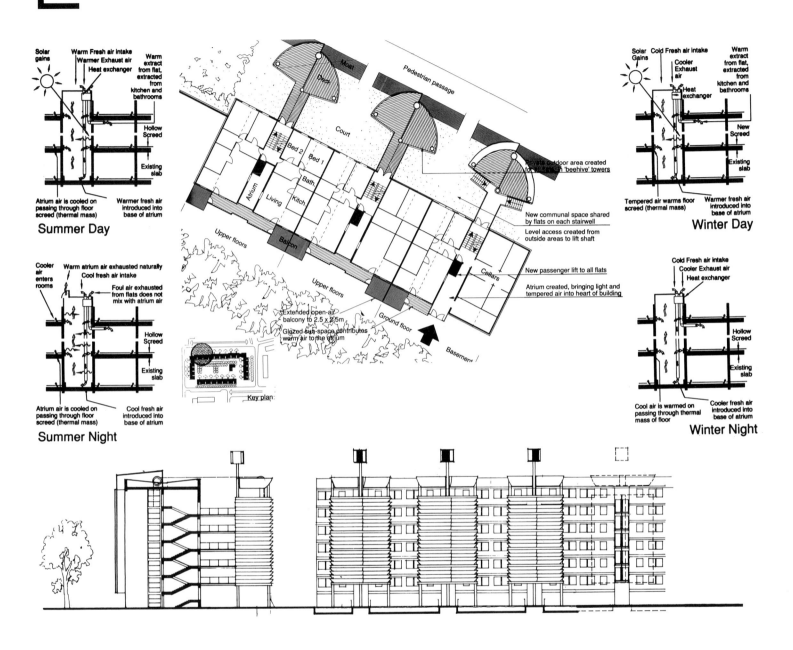

Summer Day

Solar gains
Warm Fresh air intake
Warmer Exhaust air
Heat exchanger
Warm extract from flat, extracted from kitchen and bathrooms
Hollow Screed
Existing slab
Atrium air is cooled on passing through floor screed (thermal mass)
Warmer fresh air introduced into base of atrium

Summer Night

Cooler air enters rooms
Warm atrium air exhausted naturally
Cool fresh air intake
Foul air exhausted from flats does not mix with atrium air
Hollow Screed
Existing slab
Atrium air is cooled on passing through floor screed (thermal mass)
Cool fresh air introduced into base of atrium

Winter Day

Solar Gains
Cold Fresh air intake
Cooler Exhaust air
Warm extract from flat, extracted from kitchen and bathrooms
Heat exchanger
New Screed
Existing slab
Tempered air warms floor screed (thermal mass)
Warmer fresh air introduced into base of atrium

Winter Night

Cold Fresh air intake
Cooler Exhaust air
Heat exchanger
Hollow Screed
Existing slab
Cool air is warmed on passing through thermal mass of floor
Cooler fresh air introduced into base of atrium

Moat
Dome
Court
Pedestrian passage
Bed 2
Bed 1
Bath
Atrium
Living
Kitch
Balcon
Upper floors
Upper floors
Ground floor
Cellars
Basement
Key plan

Private outdoor area created for all flats in 'beehive' towers
New communal space shared by flats on each stairwell
Level access created from outside areas to lift shaft
New passenger lift to all flats
Atrium created, bringing light and tempered air into heart of building
Extended open-air balcony to 2.5 x 2.5m
Glazed sun-space contributes warm air to the atrium

PROJECT DESCRIPTION

This project on the Berlin site creates a heirarchy of spaces from the street to the apartments. Access points to the quadrangle have been limited to improve its micro-climate and more intimate spaces at the staircase entrances are formed by the positioning of the 'beehive' towers. An atrium, the last of these spaces, has been created of the stairwells. Balconies and glazed sun-spaces are located on the south facade. 'Beehive' towers of timber, with angled blades which reflect light, give each apartment an outdoor space and support water tanks for water/wind- powered lifts. Insulated timbercladding is applied to the facades.

TECHNICAL ASSESSMENT

Overall, a good approach with some interesting ideas. The design of the atrium and sun-spaces needs development. No shading or ventilation appear to be considered, which will result in overheating in summer.

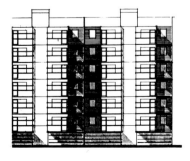

STUDENTS

1st	34B	Kai Hansen, Stephanie Heese, Jan Rützel and Anke Stollberg, Berlin, Germany	
		Technische Universitat, Berlin	72
2nd	10B	Kristian Uthe-Spencker and Laurie Baggett, Bordeaux, France	
		École d'Architecture de Bordeaux	76
3rd	58B	Petteri Piha, Helsinki, Finland	
		Helsinki University of Technology	80
4th	6B	Eva Förster, Richard Guy and Vincent Andrieu, Paris, France	
		École d'Architecture de Paris Belleville	82
Commended	13B	Christiane Fischer and Sabine Heine, Leonberg, Germany	
		École d'Architecture de Bordeaux	84
	18B	Enrique Larrumbide Gomez-Rubiera, Madrid, Spain	
		Escuela Técnica Superior de Arquitectura de Madrid	85
Exhibited	8B	Ange Leonforte, Aubagne, France	
		École d'Architecture Marseille Luminy	86
	60B	Samuli Miettinen, Tampere, Finland	
		Tampere University of Technology	87
	83B	Milica Buncáková and Stefan Onofrej, Bratislava, Slovakia	
		Slovak Technical University	88
	88B	Roswitha Kalckstein and Thomas Sigl, Vienna, Austria	
		Technical University Vienna	89
	36B	Klaus Abert, Wildflecken, Markus Hegner, Muenchberg, and Carsten Würffel, Nuedrossenfeld	
		Fachhochschule Coburg, Germany	90
	110B	Iota Aggelopoulou, Giorgos Atsalakis and Stavroula Christofilopoulou, Athens, Greece	
		National Technical University, Athens	91
	17B	Beatriz Inglès Gosàlbez, Alberto Gomez Espinosa and Javier Bernarte Paton, Madrid, Spain	
		Escuela Tècnica Superior de Arquitectura de Madrid	92

STUDENTS

1 ST PRIZE STUDENTS – 34B

Kai Hansen, Stephanie Heese, Jan Rützel and Anke Stollberg,
Technische Universitat, Berlin, Germany

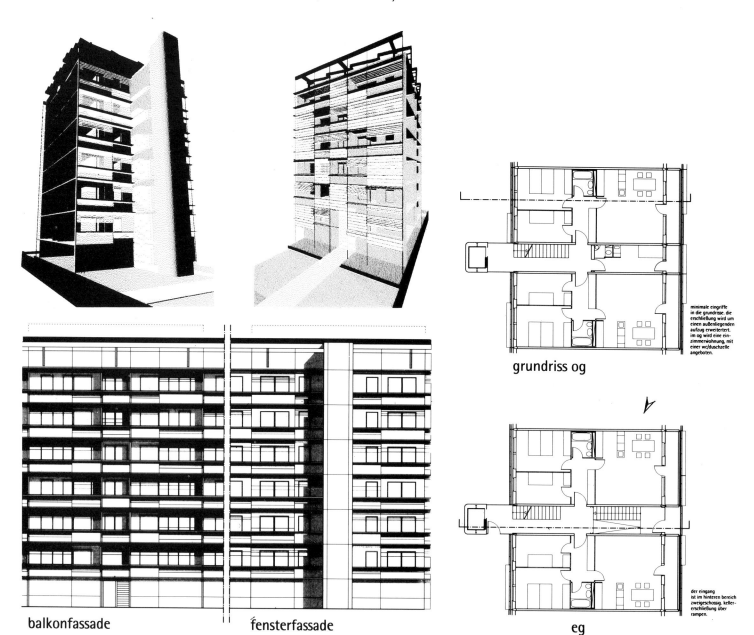

grundriss og

minimale eingriffe in die grundrisse. die erschließung wird um einen außenliegenden aufzug erweitertert. im og wird eine einzimmerwohnung, mit einer wc/duschzelle angeboten.

balkonfassade

fensterfassade

eg

der eingang ist im hinteren bereich zweigeschossig. kellererschließung über rampen.

BIOGRAPHIES

KAI HANSEN
Student at Technical Universitat, Berlin, 1991-present. Student work-experience with Grüntuch / Ernst, Berlin, 1994-95, and Stahlbau Lamparter, Kassel, 1995.

STEPHANIE HEESE
Student at Technical Universitat, Berlin, 1993-present. Student work-experience with Stahlbau Lamparter, Kassel, 1995.

PROJECT DESCRIPTION

JAN RÜTZEL
Student at Fachhochschule, Erfurt, 1991-present. Student work-experience with Stahlbau Lamparter, Kassel and HHS, Kassel, 1991, and Thomas Herzog & Partner, Munich, 1994

ANKE STOLLBERG
Student at Fachhochschule Erfurt, 1992-present. Student work-experience with Philipp Holzmann, 1993, and Bolles-Wilson, Münster, 1994.

This project, based on the Berlin site, offers a solution in the form of a device, a steel frame on the elevations which can accomodate double-glazed or transparent insulation and can be activated by users directly, or can be automated to control sun shading and prevent solar radiation reaching the building fabric.

The new facade is a steel frame attached to the roof on a 2.4m by 3.6m grid with panels at 1.2 m centres which are raised and lowered by a motorised pulley system. Several small diagrams clearly show the operation of the building under different conditions. Its use in controlling acoustic conditions indoors is questionable

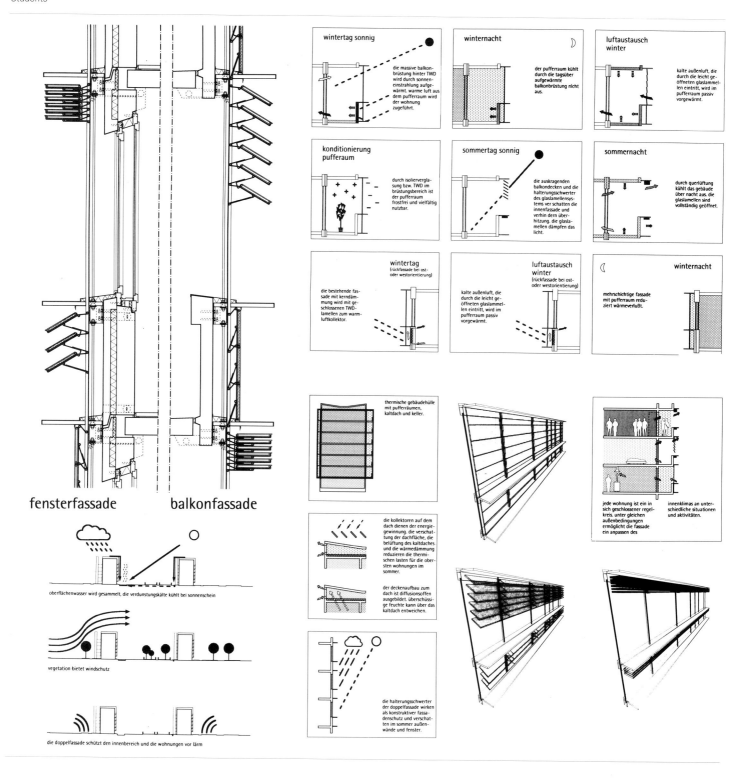

TECHNICAL ASSESSMENT

and probably is only effective when fully closed.
Interventions to the existing building are minimal. The double-stairway is combined into a single double-height space with a lift incorporated on the facade. In the apartments, kitchens are opened up to the living spaces and enlarged by the glazed balconies.

The courtyard is divided into private gardens with 'water ways' and vegetation providing a balanced micro-climate.
While the system is suitable for replication, the cost may be prohibitive.

The designers propose to create sunspaces by glazing in the balconies and improve the glazed facades by applied transparent insulation. The most dominant feature however, is the application of a sophisticated interlocking louvre system. This could be justified on the solar facades, but it is surprising to see it presented for non-

south facades.
The functioning of the balcony facades is clearer. Winter sunshine is allowed to penetrate the transparent louvres of the sunspace and provide ventilation pre-heating. It also falls on a mass element, protected by transparent insulation. In summer, the transparent louvres in a semi-parked position provide

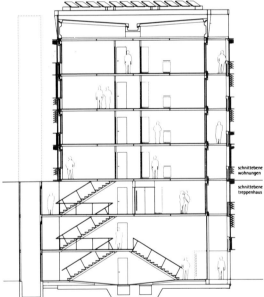

some measure of shading and the sun space is open to natural ventilation. An overhang protects the mass balustrade from the higher angled sun and the transparent insulation louvres are now full parked. Although systematically "correct" this seems a very complicated procedure. Quite evident from the beautifully presented drawings,

the louvre mechanism would be very expensive to construct and it is difficult to justify its application on such a scale. How too could appropriate operation be provided?

The existing roof is insulated externally and provided with a secondary roof which collects rain water, under which is a large ventilated cavity. An array

of solar panels provide sun-protection to the roof surface, reducing gains further in summer. Some consideration has been given to landscape and micro-climate, but this remains at a very diagrammatic level.

There is no doubt that technical design of the louvre system, and the graphic presentation is impressive; however the tech-

nical assessors considered the overall proposal to show a limited understanding of some key problems.

2ND PRIZE STUDENTS – 10B
Kristian Uthe-Spencker and Laurie Baggett, École d'Architecture de Bordeaux, France

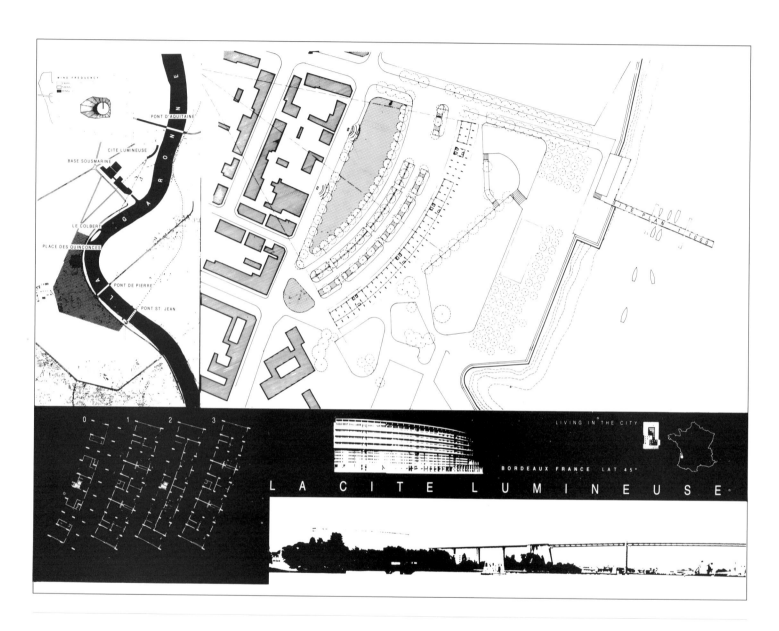

BIOGRAPHIES

KRISTIAN UTHE-SPENCKER
Vordiplom in Architecture, TU-Braunschweig, Germany, 1992. Third year Architecture, TU-Braunschweig, Germany, 1993. Student at École d'Architecture, Bordeaux, France, 1993-present.

LAURIE BAGGETT
Dip. AD (Sculpture), Liverpool College of Art, 1971.
BA. Architecture, Jesus College, Cambridge, UK.
Student at École d'Architecture, Bordeaux, France, 1993-present.

PROJECT DESCRIPTION

This project on 'La Cite Lumineuse' in Bordeaux, a fifteen story high curved apartment building built in the early 1960s on the left bank of the Garonne, is beautifully executed. It is a realistic proposal for a building that is now virtually empty and its destruction almost certain, to make way for low level housing.

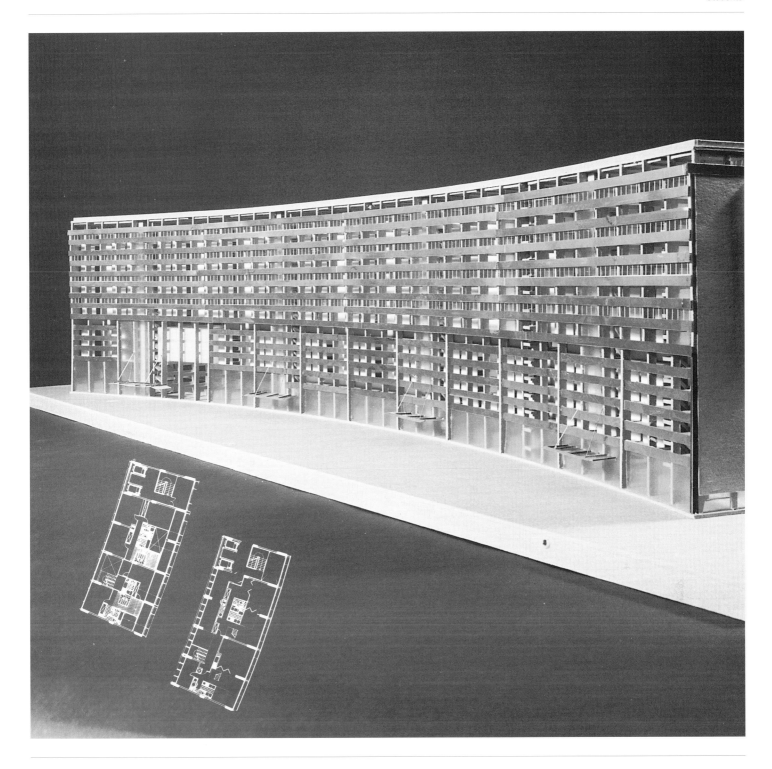

The proposals for the building combine dwellings for families and individuals with workspaces, commercial premises, roof-top restaurant and an Ecology Centre. The block is already divided into four and this division has been retained. Considerable effort has been taken to avoid the monotony which is often associated with large buildings.

Apartments have been rearranged to create duplex apartments to accomodate families and individuals. Family apartments are located in favourable positions for daytime use with the glazing lines brought forward and a sunspace at mezzanine level. A balcony at lower level gives direct contact with the Garonne and acts as a brise-soleil to the sunspace below, shading the south-east facade from oblique rays. Circulation and communal spaces have been enlarged, with amenities and social spaces added at lower levels.

As with the original construction, a systematic approach was adopted to provide flexible spaces within the limitations of the structure by the use of prefabricated elements in timber, concrete and GRC.

The quantity and quality of information provided in this student project is impressive and the treatment of the energy issues is handled convincingly.

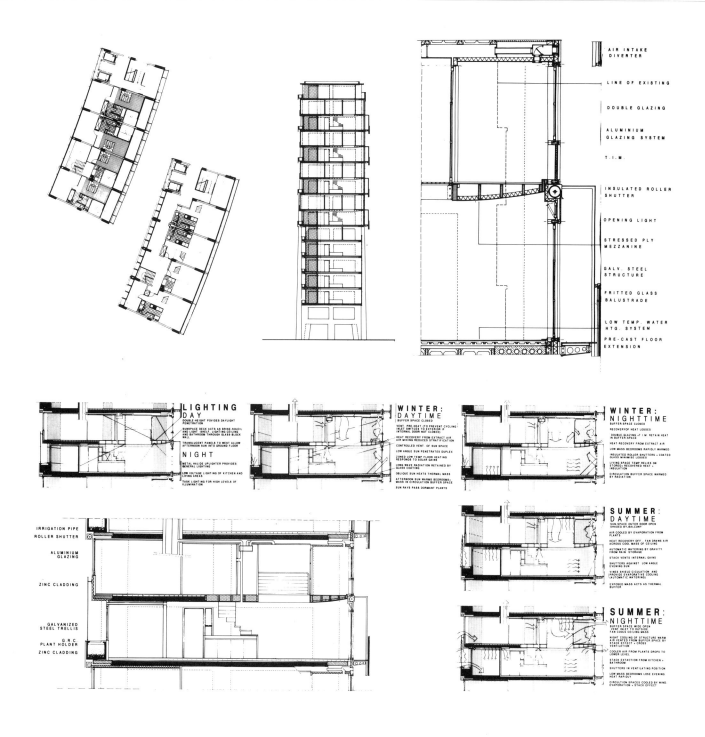

TECHNICAL ASSESSMENT

A detailed and thoughtful scheme. The SE facade is heavily modified to form a climate responsive two-storey system improving daylighting, solar gains and ventilation. Even vegetation with its own irrigation system is integrated. In the winter daytime, glazed shutters and transparent insulation allow solar gains to be made in the sunspace, whilst in the direct gain space below, sunlight penetrates to the back of the living space. At night, the direct-gain space is protected by insulated roller shutters.

In summer, the high angled sun is shaded from the sunspace, which is now open, and incoming air may receive some cooling by evaporation from plants.

There was concern by the technical assessors that the correct sun angles had been used in demonstrating the effectiveness of the shading geometry. At night, structural cooling is encouraged by air being drawn across the ceiling into a vertical stack, which also carries the outlet duct for the kitchen extract after passing through a heat recovery unit.

Underfloor heating with a relatively low water temperature is an energy-saving measure but may present control problems in spaces receiving solar gains, due to its slow response.

A very thorough energy analysis was given. Overall, this was a well-balanced and fairly realistic scheme.

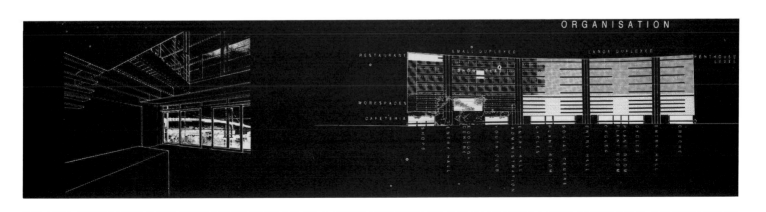

3<small>RD</small> PRIZE STUDENTS – 58B
Petteri Piha, Helsinki University of Technology, Helsinki, Finland

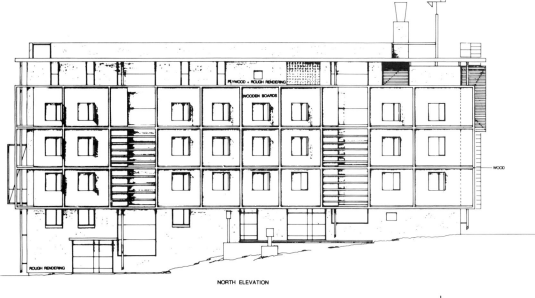

NORTH ELEVATION

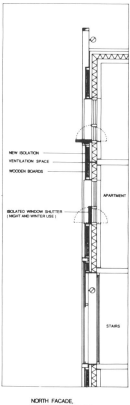

NORTH FACADE,
HORIZONTAL SECTION

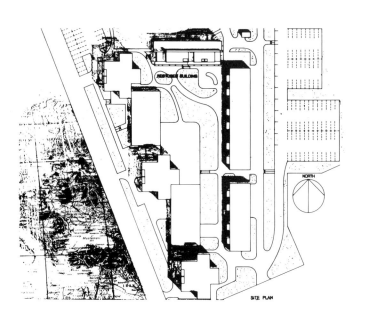

SITE PLAN

PERSPECTIVE FROM SOUTH-EAST

EXISTING VIEW FROM EAST (SHOWS ALSO THE NORTH FACADE TYPE)

PROJECT DESCRIPTION

This project is based on a four storey building in the northern part of Helsinki, built in 1967, in a wooded area. Throughout the project the environmental impact of materials has been considered. The proposal is to clad the building in timber over a new layer of insulation on the north facade, and to use wood as a structural material for the sunspace to the south facade. The sunspaces collect heat and transfer it to the central heating system. The proposed penthouse which accomodates apartments, sauna and roof-terrace, is constructed and clad in timber. Fire proofing has been considered as has transport, preservation, detailing and maintenance of the timber. The basement provides services and communal spaces.

This scheme shows a good balance of economy and innovation and is of significant architectural quality.

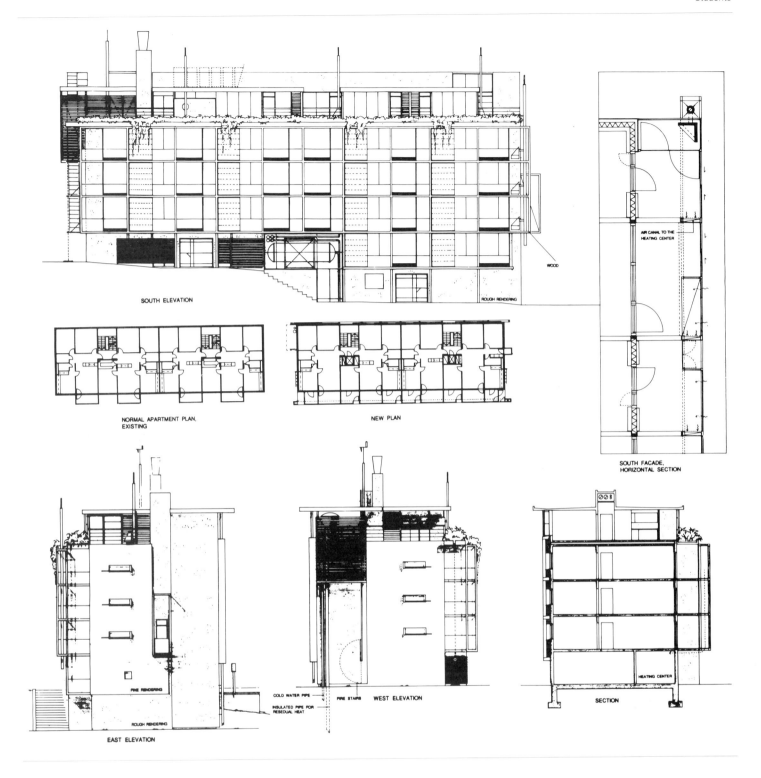

SOUTH ELEVATION

ROUGH RENDERING

WOOD

NORMAL APARTMENT PLAN,
EXISTING

NEW PLAN

AIR CANAL TO THE
HEATING CENTER

SOUTH FACADE,
HORIZONTAL SECTION

PINE RENDERING

ROUGH RENDERING

EAST ELEVATION

COLD WATER PIPE

INSULATED PIPE FOR
RESIDUAL HEAT

FIRE STAIRS   WEST ELEVATION

HEATING CENTER

SECTION

TECHNICAL ASSESSMENT

This was one of the few schemes to consider the environmental impact of materials and the architect's response was to apply external insulation protected by wood, where even the transport distance of this material was considered (although they did not actually say what the insulation material was). The north windows are also provided with insulating shutters. On the south facade, a timber structure supports a large area of sunspace, and it was a little surprising to find that this alone was relied upon to provide effective insulation. The technical assessors would have expected to find a more defensive strategy in such a cold climate as Finland.

The sunspaces act as solar collectors, ducts returning warm air to the building "energy centre". This is questionable bearing in mind the electrical fan power needed for quite small returns in thermal energy. A new penthouse floor is provided, the value of the extra space helping to offset the marginal cost of providing just roof insulation. Significant, but realistic energy use reductions were predicted.

4TH PRIZE STUDENTS – 6B

Eva Förster, Richard Guy and Vincent Andrieu,
École d'Architecture de Paris Belleville, Paris, France

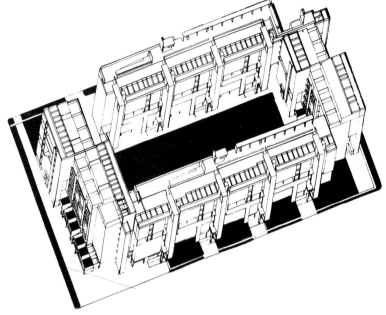

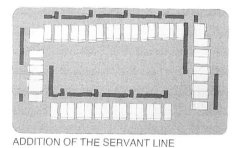

ADDITION OF THE SERVANT LINE

PROJECT DESCRIPTION

This project on the Berlin site proposes to add buffer spaces to the south, east and west facades, while adding a parallel structure to the north, east and west. The latter containing services, such as staircases, lifts, kitchens, bathrooms, pipes and conduits which allow the existing apartment areas to be used for living space. Providing a gar-den to the first floor apartments gains a space for covered carparking below.

A roof garden provides all other apartment dwellers with an outdoor space. A void is maintained between the existing and parallel structures. Although this project has not fulfilled many of the basic energy issues – such as daylighting and ventilation – it does demonstrate a redeeming architectural quality.

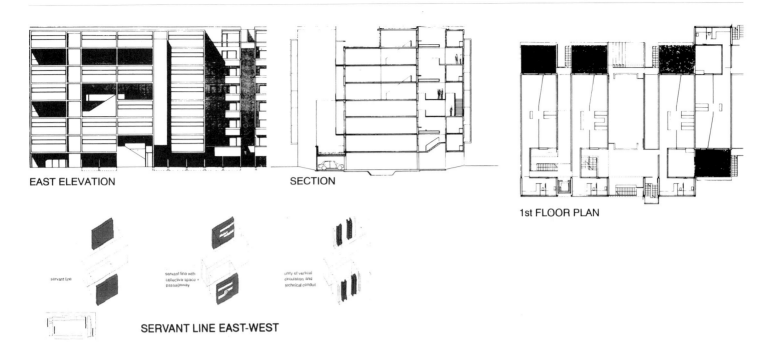

EAST ELEVATION

SECTION

1st FLOOR PLAN

servant line

servant line with collective space + passageway

unity of vertical circulation and technical conduit

SERVANT LINE EAST-WEST

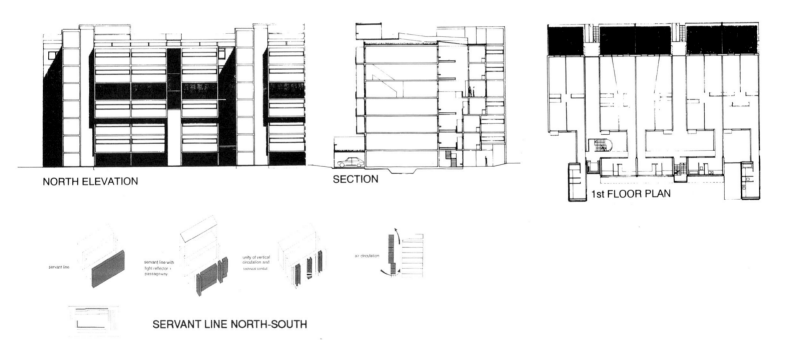

NORTH ELEVATION

SECTION

1st FLOOR PLAN

servant line

servant line with light reflector + passageway

unity of vertical circulation and technical conduit

air circulation

SERVANT LINE NORTH-SOUTH

TECHNICAL ASSESSMENT

Buffer spaces are proposed for one facade of the blocks, facing south, east and west. However, the design of these does not respond to orientation, and in any case no provision for shading or ventilation is shown. On the opposite facade to the buffer space, a free standing parallel "servant line" building which containing stairs, horizontal circulation, kitchen and bathroom is proposed, attached to the original building by bridges. This forms a kind of open-to-the-air atrium space between them.

The technical assessors were strongly critical of this on two main counts - firstly it leads to a large increase in surface area (it would be better to increase the apartment size inside the existing but thermally improved, envelope), and secondly its presence seriously degrades daylighting, and the view from the parent building. Furthermore, since it is open to the air it does nothing to solve the poor insulation of the adjacent facade. As well as these criticisms, the internal planning is not efficient in the normal sense, and the proposal has obvious economic weaknesses.

Commended Students – 13B

Christiane Fischer and Sabine Heine,
École d'Architecture de Bordeaux, France

2.a west view model

2.c communal buildings

2.d communal buildings

2.e internal corridor

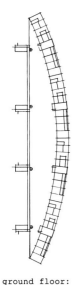

ground floor:
entrances and storages

schematic plan

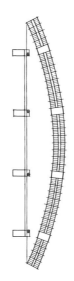

first floor:
storerooms

(other flat combinations possible)

floors 6,11:
one storey flats

floors 2,4,7,9,12,14:
two storey flats,
lower storey

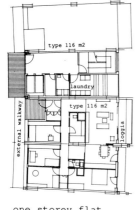

one storey flat

two storey flat,
lower storey

two storey flat,
upper storey

PROJECT DESCRIPTION

This project (the second entry submitted on 'La Cite Lumineuse' in Bordeaux) has taken a different approach by proposing the construction of four communal buildings to serve as intermediaries between 'La Cite' and the small houses surrounding it. With varying functions at different levels, including shop, nursery, workrooms and community rooms. These are accessed by external walkways and connected back to the apartment building at service areas on the north-west. Two floors of the building are one storey apartments with external walkway, others are duplex and have internal walkways.

TECHNICAL ASSESSMENT

A substantial bufferspace is created on the curved NW facade by sacrificing internal volume and creating a new internal street. This drastic and unusual measure would have the effect of improving daylight penetration and reducing heat losses from the habitable rooms, provided that the buffer space remained unheated. The SE facade has also been remodelled to form double-stacked sunspaces with rather complex shading devices and transparent insulation. There is a very thorough energy and comfort analysis using LT4.

COMMENDED STUDENTS – 18B
Enrique Larrumbide Gomez-Rubiera,
Escuela Técnica Superior de Arquitectura de Madrid, Spain

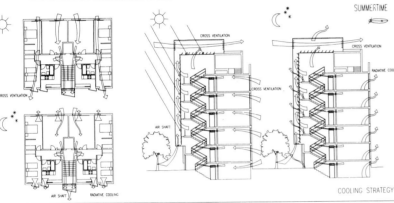

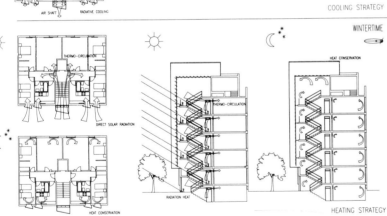

PROJECT DESCRIPTION

This project on the Pécs site is a simple and sensitive solution, which involves the distribution of smaller apartments to enlarge others, the addition of sunspaces, new windows and insulation to all facades.

All the apartments have three bedrooms and lifts have been added. Sunspaces in the form of angled bay windows are added to stairwells with glazed panels and louvres which regulate ventilation. Angled bay windows have been added to south and west with openings decreased on the north and east facades. Insulation has been added externally to walls and roofs.

TECHNICAL ASSESSMENT

The technical assessors commented on the thorough insulation details, a major contributor to energy saving in a building such as this. Ventilation was also given detailed consideration, with summer ventilation being enhanced by the stack effect via the stair-wells and the extended towers above. However, it was felt that the passive solar measures (angled glazing to bays and stairwell glazing) would give no significant energy saving. No attention was paid to shading and no overheating analysis was carried out.

EXHIBITED STUDENTS – 8B

Ange Leonforte, École d'Architecture Marseille Luminy, Marseille, France

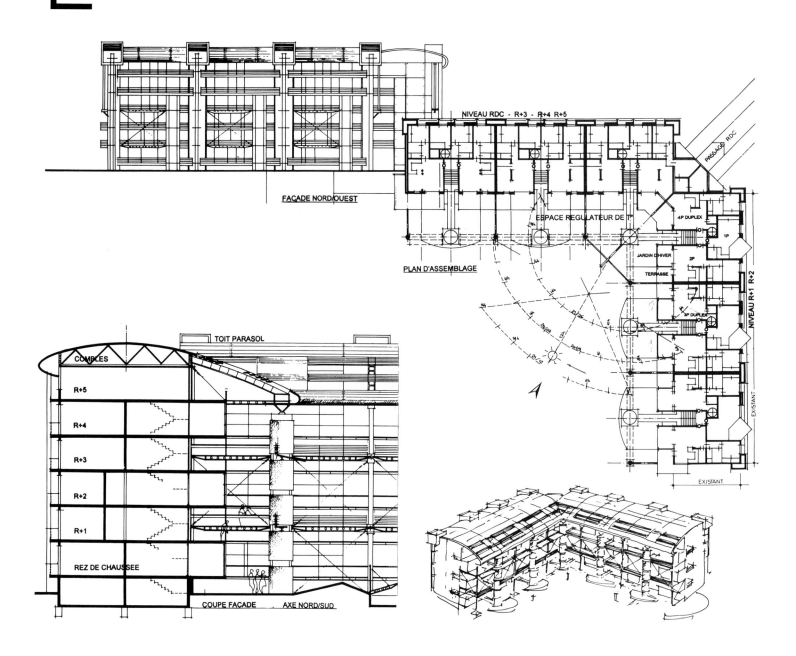

FACADE NORD/OUEST

NIVEAU RDC - R+3 - R+4 R+5

PLAN D'ASSEMBLAGE

ESPACE REGULATEUR DE T°

TOIT PARASOL

COMBLES

R+5

R+4

R+3

R+2

R+1

REZ DE CHAUSSEE

COUPE FACADE   AXE NORD/SUD

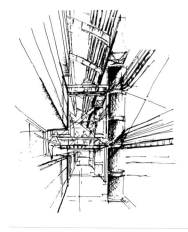

PROJECT DESCRIPTION

This project based on the Pécs site creates an additional structure independant of the existing building, in steel, with a 'parasol roof', in the form of an aeroplane wing which forms a semi-private buffer space, and includes the lifts. Sunspaces within the space enlarge the apartment and can be regulated with ventilation grilles and vertical shutters according to personal preference. Apartments are rearranged to have living spaces to the south west and bedrooms to the north east. Ventilated external insulation is added to north and east facades. By adding an additional storey, in lightweight materials, the number of apartments remains unchanged.

TECHNICAL ASSESSMENT

Excellent analysis, strategy and level of innovation.

The large overhang, whilst providing shading and some protection from rain and wind, would not provide a thermally improved micro-climate. It is not clear that the ventilation patterns as shown, would be achieved.

E XHIBITED STUDENTS – 60B

Samuli Miettinen, Tampere University of Technology, Finland

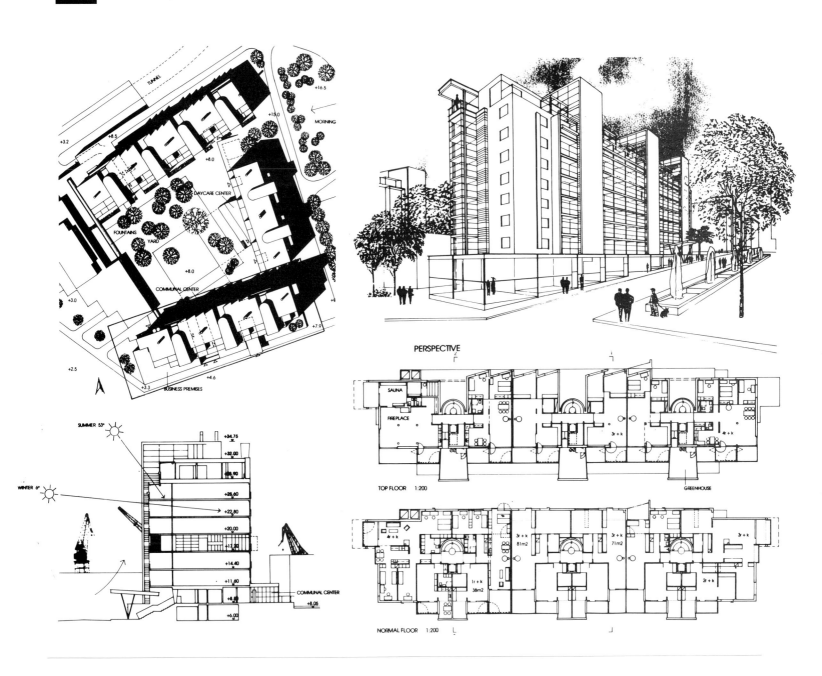

PERSPECTIVE

SAUNA

FIREPLACE

TOP FLOOR 1:200

GREENHOUSE

NORMAL FLOOR 1:200

PROJECT DESCRIPTION

This project on the harbour side in Helsinki, originally built in 1970. It aims to reorganise the apartments spatially, to increase / optimise solar energy and to orient the apartments to their surroundings giving views of the sea and parks, and integrating them into the industrial architecture of the area.

The existing living spaces and balconies on the north are reorganised to the south with balconies forming a continuous winter garden facing the park. At roof level additional apartments and communal areas with fireplaces and saunas are provided. A daycare and community centre are located on the ground level with commercial activities at street level.

TECHNICAL ASSESSMENT

A well analysed and presented practical solution with high replication potential. Some aspects of the configuration of the solar systems, such as the south facade of the sunspace could be improved.

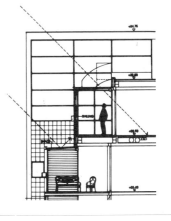

E XHIBITED STUDENTS – 83B

Milica Buncáková and Stefan Onofrej
Slovak Technical University, Bratislava, Slovakia

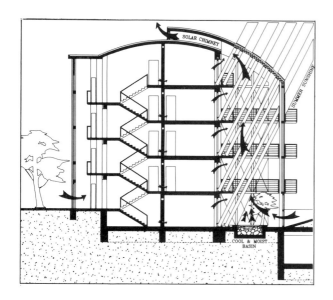

STREET PERSPECTIVE

COURT PERSPECTIVE

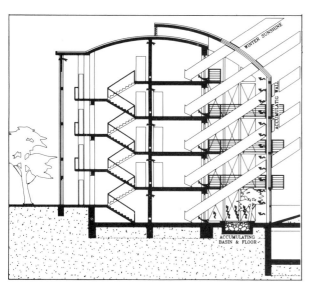

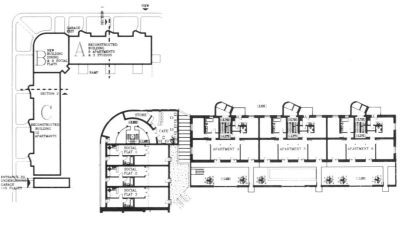

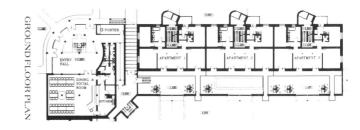

GROUND FLOOR PLAN

PROJECT DESCRIPTION

This project for a typical three-storey apartment building in Krasnany, Bratislava, fills in the corner between two buildings with an entrance space, which includes social rooms, cafes and apartments. The existing apartment building is re-arranged to double the size of the apartments, provide lifts at the street face and a sunspace to the courtyard permitting passive cooling in the summer and heating in the winter. Studios are located on the roof and service areas providing storage, washing and drying facilities are located in the basement. Carparking is provided underneath the courtyard.

TECHNICAL ASSESSMENT

This project represents a good overall approach, with good potential for replication; however some areas such as cooling and ventilation of the sunspace would need to be treated in greater depth. Good architectural integration is evident.

E XHIBITED STUDENTS – 88B

Roswitha Kalckstein and Thomas Sigl, Technical University Vienna, Austria

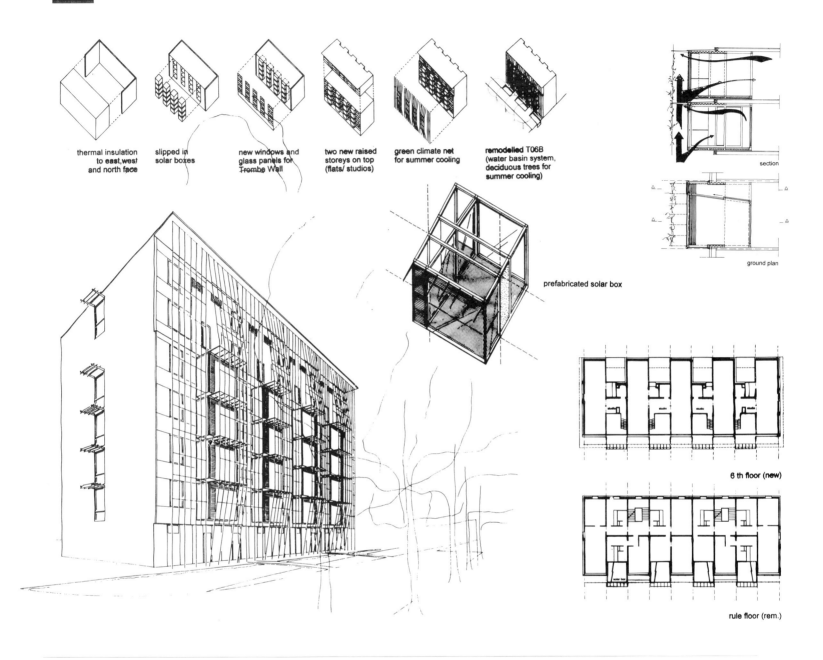

thermal insulation to east, west and north face

slipped in solar boxes

new windows and glass panels for Trombe Wall

two new raised storeys on top (flats/ studios)

green climate net for summer cooling

remodelled T06B (water basin system, deciduous trees for summer cooling)

prefabricated solar box

section

ground plan

6 th floor (new)

rule floor (rem.)

PROJECT DESCRIPTION

This project for an apartment building in the north-west of Kaplice, Czech Republic, built in the 1960s, provides a thorough energy and cost analyis of the solution. Prefabricated 'solar boxes' are inserted into the south facade in place of the existing concrete panels to provide solar gains in winter. A green 'climatic net' for deciduous vegetation provides cooling in summer. New double glazed units are installed and existing single glazed units are mounted on concrete parapets to provide a trombe wall effect. North, east and west facades are clad in cork insulation with smaller double-glazed windows. Two new stories at roof level provide apartments and studios.

TECHNICAL ASSESSMENT

Very thorough energy and cost analysis with clear step-by-step strategy for remodelling, which includes external insulation, 'solar-box' units with green climate nets for vegitation growth and trombe walls are proposed. Technical details need to be improved.

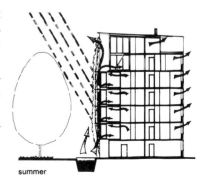

summer

E XHIBITED STUDENTS – 36B

Klaus Abert, Markus Hegner and Carsten Würffel
Fachhochschule Coburg, Germany

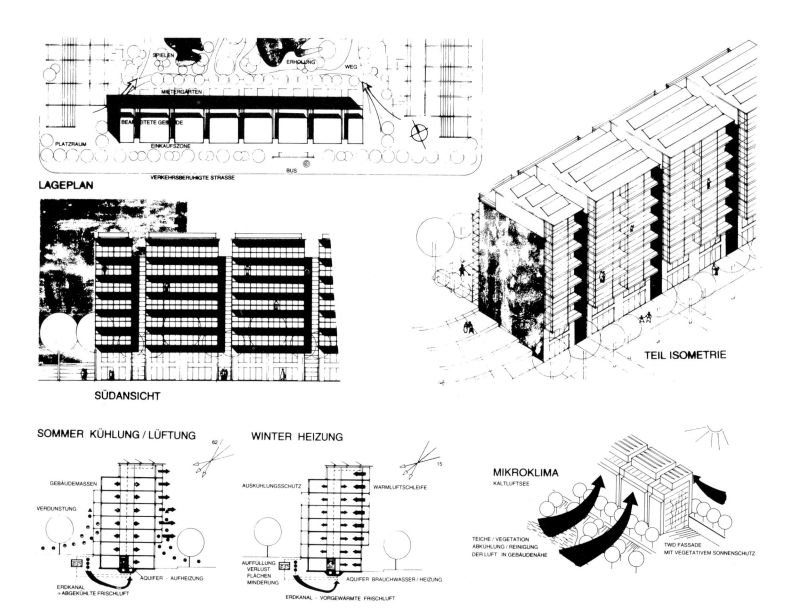

LAGEPLAN

SÜDANSICHT

TEIL ISOMETRIE

SOMMER KÜHLUNG / LÜFTUNG

WINTER HEIZUNG

MIKROKLIMA

PROJECT DESCRIPTION

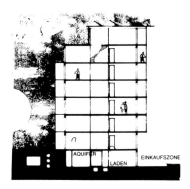

This project on the Berlin site, in contrast to others, opens up the courtyard to connect it to the street, which is heavily planted with trees. A shopping area is proposed for the ground level of the south block. East and west buildings are extended.

The apartments are redesigned as open plan with buffer spaces on both facades enlarging the apartments. With solar collectors on east and west facades and floors heated by solar radiation, winter comfort is greatly enhanced.

TECHNICAL ASSESSMENT

The spatial arrangement in this entry is satisfactory, with the addition of buffer spaces to both facades, but the elevational treatment is unresolved architecturally. Well-elaborated technical details of winter and summer comfort.

EXHIBITED STUDENTS – 110B

Iota Aggelopoulou, Giorgos Atsalakis and Stavroula Christofilopoulou,
National Technical University, Athens, Greece

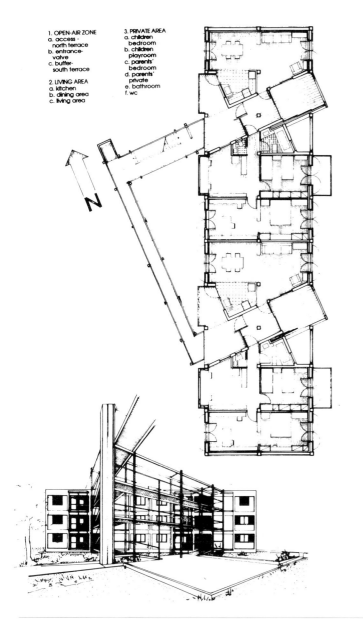

1. OPEN-AIR ZONE
a. access - north terrace
b. entrance-valve
c. buffer-south terrace

2. LIVING AREA
a. kitchen
b. dining area
c. living area

3. PRIVATE AREA
a. children bedroom
b. children playroom
c. parents' bedroom
d. parents' private
e. bathroom
f. wc

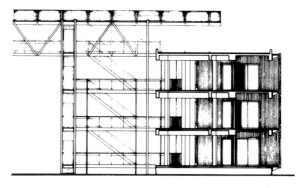

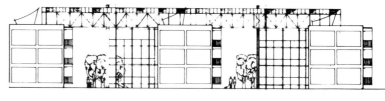

PROJECT DESCRIPTION

This project is based on a 1957 housing complex in Pireaus, Greece. Because of east / west orientation, ventilation from the north winds is not possible, resulting in overheating in summer. To combat this, a north / south metal structure has been added to the building in the form of an access zone which penetrates the building and connects with the roof terrace. It also provides a structure for devices to shade the west elevation The reorganisation of the plan to accommodate this results in two larger apartments on each floor, with a south-facing balcony, which in winter months forms a buffer space. Walls are insulated and double-glazed windows are provided.

TECHNICAL ASSESSMENT

The architectural approach of cutting and interconnecting the three buildings with a metal structure is interesting , but the cost implications are not conducive to replication. Daylighting and air quality issues have been addressed, but no calculations for over-heating are provided.

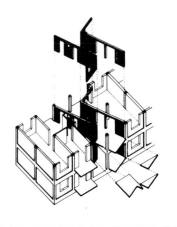

EXHIBITED STUDENTS – 17B

*Beatriz Inglés Gosálbez, Alberto Gomez Espinosa and Javier Bernarte Paton,
Escuela Técnica Superior de Arquitectura de Madrid, Spain*

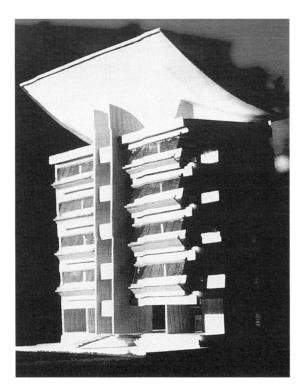

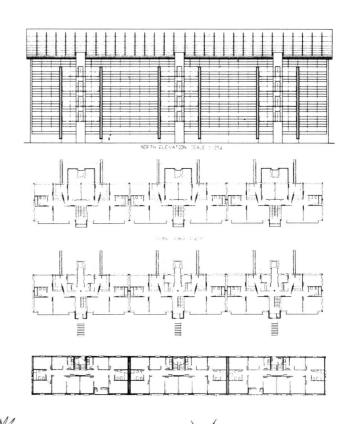

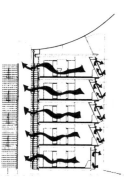
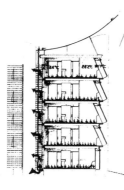
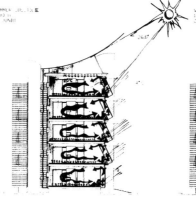
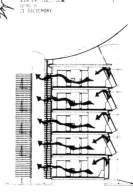

PROJECT DESCRIPTION

This project in Puertolland, Spain, is orientated north-south but because of small window openings does not make any significant use of passive solar energy. Re-organisation of the plan moves the kitchens and bathrooms towards the north, with living spaces to the south. Lift access is also on the north. The south facade is converted into a solar collector with horizontal sunshading, angled glass and screen to protect from overheating in summer. An arched roof provides cool water on summer nights which flows to the floor for cooling in summer and is heated by solar gains from under the window in winter time. Cross ventilation is provided.

TECHNICAL ASSESSMENT

This project shows an imaginative and interesting but complex overall approach, which would require additional technical information for implementation. The roof structure structure may be too extravagent for replication and no cost analysis is included.

THE FOLLOWING ENTRIES WERE SELECTED BY THE
ARCHITECTURAL JURY FOR SPECIAL MENTION

Architects

5A   Studio E Architects Limited, London, United Kingdom
21A   Héléne Mehats Grutter and Alexandre Grutter,
        Strasbourg, France
55A   Roberto Grio, Rome, Italy
106A   Wojciech Korbel, Cracow, Poland
46A   Judith Ubarrechena, L2M Architects, San Sebastian,
        Spain
124A   Dimitris Polychronopoulos, Matina Georgopoulou and
        George Kontoroupis, Athens, Greece
33A   Andrew Holmes, Paris, France
80A   Karel Vandenhende, Gent, Belgium
61A   Prof. Sergio Croce, Prof. Emilio Pizzi & others, Milan, Italy
36A   Florence Champiot and Isabelle Ducos, Bordeaux, France
91A   Mari Duffner, Frankfurt, Valeria Retamal-Pucheu,
        Hamburg, Germany
22A   Philippe Lamarque and Pierre Guillot, Bordeaux, France

Students

8B   Ange Leonforte,
        Ecole d'Architecture Marseille Luminy, France
60B   Samuli Miettinen,
        Tampere University of Technology, Helsinki, Finland
83B   Milica Buncáková and Stefan Onofrej,
        Slovak Technical University, Bratislava, Slovakia
88B   Roswitha Kalckstein and Thomas Sigl,
        Technical University Vienna, Austria
36B   Klaus Abert, Markus Hegner, Carsten Würffel,
        Fachhochschule Coburg, Germany
110B   Iota Aggelopoulou, Giorgos Atsalakis, Stavroula
        Christofilopoulou
        National Technical University, Athens, Greece
17B   Beatriz Inglés Gosálbez, Alberto Gomez Espinosa, Javier
        Bernarte Paton,
        Escuela Técnica Superior de Arquitectura de Madrid,
        Spain
20B   Susana Rodriguez Garcia, Patricia Pintado Casas, Rafael
        Gomez Martinez,
        Escuela Técnica Superior de Arquitectura de Madrid,
        Spain
30B   Atelier 'Ap-Art', Uta Kleffling, Stefan Paulisch, Ralph
        Riesmeier, Apolda, Germany
94B   Vladimir Velinov,
        University of Architecture, Civil Engineering and
        Geodesy, Sofia, Bulgaria
98B   Marko Peterlin,
        University of Ljubljana, Slovenia

THE FOLLOWING ENTRIES WERE SELECTED BY THE
TECHNICAL ASSESSORS FOR SPECIAL MENTION

Architects

95A   Rob Marsh, Büro-E, Copenhagen, Denmark
5A   Studio E Architects Limited, London, United Kingdom
25A   Delta Architectes SA, Annecy, France
8A   Brian Jones, York, United Kingdom
26A   Novae Architectes, Lyon, France
43A   Martin Mulligan and others, Junglinster, Luxembourg
79A   Pierre Sauveur, Liege, Belgium
129A   **Мохорев Евгений Дмитриевич, Владимир, Россия**
110A   Henrich Pifko and Peter Matiasovsky, Bratislava,
       Slovakia
46A   Judith Ubarrechena, L2M Architects, San Sebastian,
       Spain

Students

8B   Ange Leonforte,
       Ecole d'Architecture Marseille Luminy, France
60B   Samuli Miettinen,
       Tampere University of Technology, Finland
86B   Ivan Redi, Andrea Schröttner,
       Technical University Graz, Austria
88B   Roswitha Kalckstein and Thomas Sigl,
       Technical University Vienna, Austria
83B   Milica Buncáková and Stefan Onofrej,
       Slovak Technical University, Bratislava, Slovakia
10B   Kristian Uthe-Spencker and Laurie Baggett,
       Ecole d'Architecture de Bordeaux, France
36B   Klaus Abert, Markus Hegner, Carsten Würffel,
       Fachhochschule Coburg, Germany
3B   Paul Martin Sandford,
       South Bank University, London, United Kingdom

BIBLIOGRAPHY

Other publications on the same subject matter include:

The ECD Partnership
SOLAR ARCHITECTURE IN EUROPE
Prism Press, 2 South Street, Bridport, Dorset DT6 3NQ, UK,
for EC DGXII 1991, EUR 12738 EN. ISBN 1 85327 0733.
Also published by Uitgeverij Jan van Arkel, A Numankade 17,
K P Utercht. ISBN 90 6224 998 1, and as
ARCHITECTURES SOLAIRES EN EUROPE
Edisud, La Calade RN7, 13090 Aix en Provence, France,
for EC DGXII, 1991, EUR 12738 FR. ISBN 2 85744 5181

J O Lewis & J R Goulding (Eds)
EUROPEAN DIRECTORY OF SUSTAINABLE
ENERGY-EFFICIENT BUILDING 1995
– Components, Materials, Services
James & James (Science Publishers) Ltd, 47 Kentish Town Road,
London NW1 8NZ, UK, 1996, ISBN 1 873936 486

J R Goulding, J O Lewis & T C Steemers (Eds)
ENERGY CONSCIOUS DESIGN – A PRIMER FOR ARCHITECTS
B T Batsford Ltd. 4 Fitzharding Street, London W1H 0AH, UK,
for EC DGXII, 1992, EUR 13445, ISBN 0 7134 69196

J R Goulding, J O Lewis & T C Steemers (Eds)
ENERGY IN ARCHITECTURE
– THE EUROPEAN PASSIVE SOLAR HANDBOOK
B T Batsford Ltd, London, UK,
for EC DGXII, 1992, EUR 13446, ISBN 0 7134 69188

J R Goulding, J O Lewis (Eds)
PASSIVE SOLAR RESOURCE GUIDE
A guide to publications, design tools and other aids to passive
solar design for European Architects. On 3.5" computer disc for
use on Apple Macintosh with Hypercard.
Energy Research Group, University College Dublin
for EC DG XII, 1993

N V Baker, A Fanchiotti & K Steemers (Eds)
DAYLIGHTING IN ARCHTECTURE
A European reference book.
James & James (Science Publishers) Ltd, London, UK,
for EC DGXII, 1996, ISBN 1 873936 21 4

C den Ouden & T C Steemers (Eds)
BUILDING 2000, volumes 1 and 2
32 design studies of large buildings.
Kluwer Academic Publishers, P O Box 322, 3300 AH Dirdrecht,
The Netherlands, for EC DGXII, EUR 13958 EN

E O'Cofaigh, J Olley & J O Lewis
THE CLIMATIC DWELLING
James & James (Science Publishers) Ltd, London, UK,
for EC DGXII, 1995, EUR 16615, ISBN 1 873936 486

VIDEOS

University College Dublin
DAYLIGHTING
for EC DGXVII, 1994

David Clarke Associates, London
SOLAR ARCHITECTURE IN EUROPE
Introduction to Solar Architecture. Available in VHS PAL/SECAM.
Energy Research Group, University College Dublin,
for EC DGXII, 1988

COMPETITIONS

R M Lebens
PASSIVE SOLAR ARCHITECTURE IN EUROPE
The results of the first EC Passive Solar competition, 1980.
Architectural Press, London, UK

R M Lebens
PASSIVE SOLAR ARCHITECTURE IN EUROPE 2
The results of the second EC Passive Solar competition, 1982.
Architectural Press, London, UK

S O'Toole & J O Lewis (Eds)
WORKING IN THE CITY
The results of the third EC architectural ideas competition, 1990.
Eblana Editions, Dublin, for EC DGXII, 1990, EUR 12919EN,
ISBN 0 946846 022.

D McClean, E Fitzgerald & J O Lewis (Eds)
ZEPHYR
The results of the fourth EC architectural ideas competition, 1995.
Energy Research Group, University College Dublin
for EC DGXII, 1995, EUR 16480, ISBN 1 898473 26 9

EXHIBITIONS

Energy Research Group, University College Dublin
THE ENERGY CONSCIOUS TRADITION
An exhibition in the form of 16 Posters and a catalogue.
Available in each of the nine EC languages for educational,
professional or public exhibition.
for EC DGXII, 1989

Energy Research Group, University College Dublin
/ Architectural Association Graduate School, London
/ Université Catholique de Louvain, Louvain-la-Neuve
SOLAR ARCHITECTURE – RESOURCE MATERIAL
3 portfolios of information on the climatic design of residential,
educational and tertiary architecture, for EC DGXII, 1995